Consuming Credit

DEBT & POVERTY IN THE UK

Janet Ford

CPAG Ltd, 1-5 Bath

D1396310

ISBN 0 946744 32 7

The views expressed in this book do not necessarily represent those of the Child Poverty Action Group

Cover and design by Devious Designs, 0742 755634
Typeset by Nancy White
Printed by Calvert's Press, 31-39 Redchurch Street, London E2 7DJ

CONTENTS

LIST OF TABLES
AND FIGURES

FOREWORD

The last twenty years have seen the 'glamorisation of credit', 'taking the waiting out of wanting', 'that'll do nicely', 'says more about you than money ever can'. It all seemed so effortless and desirable, and doubtless, for some, it was. Unfortunately, for the less well off, the reality was often far harsher. Credit for money was an unwanted but necessary evil, better only than the alternative – electricity disconnection, eviction and going without Christmas presents for the children.

Janet Ford addresses the use of credit of that poorer section of society in a meticulous and serious fashion. In doing so, she avoids one of the pitfalls of the credit debate of the 1980s – the moral panic. For some, credit verges on the sinful, sapping the moral fibre of the nation. Indeed, the language used sometimes refers to credit as if it were an addiction – 'credit card junkies', 'credit binges'. Again, the reality is usually less dramatic – simply that of ordinary mortals struggling to reconcile the irreconcilable.

Credit made available to poor people is expensive. To some extent this is inevitable – payments may be collected door to door in small weekly amounts in a labour intensive fashion. But it is also expensive because of the market position of poor borrowers – deprived of alternative sources, often desperate for a loan to avert some domestic catastrophe, with no margin in their weekly income, they are vulnerable to extortionate rates of charge. The existing laws designed to prevent extortionate lending have been ineffective.

This study vividly portrays the patterns of credit use in a detailed and factual way. Particular aspects, however, stand out. First, is the extent to which the bargaining with creditors, the managing within the household, the balancing of commitments is overwhelmingly carried out by women. Second, because families with children have the most unpredictable calls on their budgets, they are particularly vulnerable when it comes to incurring commitments. Again, this responsibility falls overwhelmingly on women.

The book ends by looking forward. Credit does not have to be a scourge – indeed, for many people who read this book, it is not. It can be a way of spreading commitments quite sensibly, sometimes over very long terms. There is the need for new lending institutions operating in the interests of poorer people. Credit unions are a start and there are examples from which we can learn in other European countries. But Janet Ford reminds us that time and again a major influence on debt is purely and simply poverty. If that were alleviated, many of our problems of indebtedness would solve themselves.

Robin Simpson
Deputy Director of the National Consumer Council
Writing as a Member of CPAG's Executive Committee

ACKNOWLEDGMENTS

I would like to thank the following people or organisations for allowing tables from their publications to be reproduced: Saul Becker and Richard Silburn, Richard Berthoud and Elaine Kempson, Birmingham City Council, Birmingham Settlement Money Advice Centre, the National Consumer Council, the Office of Fair Trading and Public Attitude Surveys, and Michael Saunders. In addition, particular thanks are due to those people within CPAG, along with other friends and colleagues, who made detailed and valuable comments on the manuscript. Fran Bennett, Richard Kennedy and Julia Lewis have undertaken all the production work and I am particularly grateful to them.

INTRODUCTION
AND OVERVIEW

By the end of the 1980s, 75 per cent of households in Britain had access to credit facilities.[1] As a percentage of personal disposable income, personal sector net borrowing for consumer credit (including mortgages) rose from 7 per cent in the late 1970s to 17 per cent in 1989.[2] The pattern of repayment of credit also changed. Up until the late 1970s, households (in aggregate) repaid more each year than they took in new borrowing. Subsequently, households have taken a greater amount of new credit each year than has been repaid, and the level of personal indebtedness has therefore risen. The increase has been both an absolute and a real increase.[3]

Individuals and households use credit for a variety of reasons and with different implications. The particular concern of this book is low-income borrowers and the extent to which the links between poverty, credit and debt have tightened over the recent past. This theme is pursued with reference to existing published material.

In this book, 'credit' refers to any form of loan. However, although technically everyone using credit is 'in debt' because money is owed, if payments are made when they fall due this type of debt is not problematic. Thus, the term 'debt' is used here to refer to any situation in which due payments have not been made. In other words, debt equals default or arrears.

Low-income households use credit considerably less than affluent households and it tends to be associated with necessity rather than choice. Furthermore, over most of the twentieth century the pattern of access to credit by those living in poverty has been both restricted and costly. Credit use amongst low-income households arises for several reasons, one of which is the need to bridge the gulf between inadequate resources and basic requirements. In the nineteenth and early twentieth century, poor households turned to pawnbrokers, money-lenders or tallymen (doorstep traders) to bridge this gulf. Recent studies have presented evidence of continuing poverty in the United Kingdom, and the inadequacy of the resources available to many low-income households in relation to their needs.[4] Such households continue to seek additional resources in order to provide a basic standard of living, and one option open to them is to borrow.

> It is hard for many, and impossible for some – particularly families with dependent children on the basic rates – to maintain reasonably decent standards for any appreciable length of time without help from other sources. For them, life on supplementary benefit is a bleak struggle to make ends meet.[5]

However, during the 1980s, there were additional factors which increased the use of credit amongst all groups, but had particular significance for low-income households. For example, an increasing number of low-income households were drawn into home ownership, particularly as a result of the 'right to buy' council homes policy. There was also a shift in some policy areas from providing support to people in the form of grants, to offering credit agreements (for example, with the development of the social fund loan system for claimants, or student loans). Many of these developments were the result of government policies introduced following the election of the Thatcher Government in 1979 and interact with a further aspect of government policy in the early 1980s – the deregulation of financial markets – which altered the credit environment for borrowers and lenders and was at the heart of the increase in the availability of credit in the 1980s. As controls on lending were successively removed, competition between creditors grew (not least because lending in the personal sector offered substantial opportunities for growth in contrast to the emerging problems with lending to the Third World or domestic industry) and credit has been intensively marketed in the attempt to secure borrowers. People who had been previously excluded from most if not all of the credit market (because they lacked the necessary deposit or security) found a greater number of opportunities open to them. These changes are discussed in more detail in Chapter 1.

Low-income borrowers are particularly vulnerable to debt

simply because their resources are low and inadequate. In addition, debts often emerge in the absence of credit, as is the case with fuel or rent arrears. As access to credit broadened during the 1980s (however limited this was for those living in poverty), and the amount of credit taken or number of agreements entered increased, unless households had some additional resources they became ever more vulnerable. This vulnerability has been accentuated by a further set of factors, many of which impinge particularly heavily on low-income households – unemployment, the growth of low-wage casual work and the central role of the interest-rate mechanism in the management of the economy that can produce rapid changes in the costs of credit.

Chapter 1 examines the growing link between poverty and credit. The reasons for the growth of poverty in the 1980s are discussed – in particular the impact of unemployment, the growth of casual low-paid work and the changes in the social security system that have reduced the welfare benefits available to some of those living in poverty. All of these factors increase the likelihood that households caught in these situations will have to seek credit to manage their poverty. Evidence is discussed in order to establish the degree to which low-income households use credit, the extent to which there has been any change in the level of use and the forms of credit used. The importance of credit in the expansion of low-income home ownership is also considered. The discussion of low-income credit is set in the context of the broader trends in credit use and availability, and a consideration of those processes that have been implicated in the exceptional growth in credit in the 1980s.

The restricted financial position of poor households seeking credit is exacerbated by the organisation of the commercial credit market. Unequal access to credit and its differential costs are discussed in Chapter 2. Poor borrowers are excluded from some forms of credit and are channelled into a high-cost market for others. The poorest borrowers tend to use mail order, check trading and money-lenders, while other low-income borrowers also have mortgage credit and finance house loans (these different forms of credit are explained in the Glossary at the end of the book). In addition, credit is available from family and friends and from the social fund. The relationships between the cost of credit, access, affordability and collection processes suggest that, in many cases – with the very important exception of cost – most forms of low-income commercial credit are structured to reflect the needs and constraints of low-income budgeting. There is a clear contrast with the social fund budgeting and crisis loans. These loans are available only to the very poorest. With the exception of cost (these loans are interest free) such loans constitute a credit system that largely fails to connect with the realities of low-income budgeting and in practice frequently operates to increase the need of low-income families to turn to the commercial credit market.

As the incidence and extent of poverty grew through the 1980s, so did the use of credit by low-income households. Debt also increased, and Chapter 3 highlights the concentration of debt amongst the poor and shows the particular vulnerability to debt of low-income households with children. Debts are substantial with regard to rent, finance company loans, fuel, check trading, money-lenders and the poll tax, but there is also mortgage and hire purchase default. Their exclusion from certain types of credit is considerable, however, with the result that few, if any, of the poor owe on bank loans, overdrafts, store or credit cards. The evidence concerning the social and personal costs of debt is also examined in Chapter 3. Social isolation, the retention of the problems within the household and conflicts about the causes and appropriate response to debt are noted, along with the pressure to borrow further to try to solve the problems. The process by which borrowers both seek and are sought by creditors who specialise in loans to the indebted is discussed as one that involves even greater costs and higher risks for borrowers and potentially high profits for the lenders.

Chapter 4 considers the growing extent to which women are affected by poverty and debt. Women are more likely to experience poverty as a result of their position in society. They are either excluded from the labour market altogether, or typically assigned poor jobs. In addition, society places little value on what is regarded as their primary role – childcare and homemaking. One group of women particularly at risk of poverty are lone mothers, who provide a focus for the discussion. Lone mothers form a growing number of those living on benefit and experience some of the highest levels of need. A higher proportion of lone mothers have multiple credit commitments than have other groups of claimants, and they also have high levels of debt, particularly for rent and fuel. To a greater extent than many other claimants, lone mothers are involved with the social fund and thus prone to the difficulties that stem from that form of credit - ie, inflexible budgeting processes, further debt and the pressure to use additional commercial credit. Within households comprised of couples, women may also be poor where they are responsible for domestic management within a pattern of household financial allocation that makes insufficient resources available to them. Chapter 4 goes on to discuss the impact of different forms of household financial allocation on women's need to take credit and manage debt, and also notes that, irrespective of the pattern of financial allocation, once debt exists, women are the principal managers of the debt negotiation and debt recovery processes.

Chapters 1 to 4 indicate in different ways the links between poverty, credit and debt and also the vulnerability and exploitation of poor households in the credit market. Chapter 5 examines the protection afforded credit users in law, particularly, but not exclusively, with regard to extortionate and/or illegal credit agreements and debt recovery processes. While in principle protection exists, the practice is somewhat different. A dearth of economic resources and lack of knowledge and familiarity with the legal procedures partly account for the ineffectiveness of this protection. However, it is equally the case that the current availability of credit to the poor is so restricted that there exists a measure of collusion between borrowers and high cost, even extortionate, creditors in so far as, from the borrowers' perspective, costly credit is better than no credit at all. Only when there is choice with regard to credit sources will the law have a chance to function more effectively with regard to protecting those most disadvantaged in the credit market.

Under current circumstances, poor households are becoming increasingly involved in multiple credit and debt problems with little available to them in the way of help or information. Support for the indebted in the form of money advice is discussed and found to be growing, but still limited and hampered by a fragile funding base. However, money advice is not seen as unproblematic. Access is constrained and the process has to take account of conflicts between creditors as well as between creditors and borrowers. Borrowers and creditors may evaluate the usefulness of the service in different ways.

Chapter 6 briefly considers some of the further issues and implications that arise from the preceding chapters, in particular the need for a low income credit system and for a form of debt recovery that is more responsive to the needs of the borrower.

This publication has its origins in *Unemployment, Credit and Debt in Britain,* a report that was prepared for a European conference held in Hamburg in September 1989. That report was jointly produced by a number of people (Pat Conaty, Simon Johnson, John Kruse, Phil Woodall and myself). Although the theme and scope of this publication are different, their help and input have been important. So too have the comments of a number of CPAG readers. I am, however, solely responsible for the views presented here.

NOTES

1. R Berthoud and E Kempson, *Credit and Debt in Britain: First Findings,* Policy Studies Institute, 1990.
2. M Saunders, *The Coming Decline in Personal Sector Borrowing,* Greenwell Montagu Research Paper, 1988.
3. *Banking World,* April 1986.
4. C Oppenheim, *Poverty: The Facts,* CPAG Ltd, 1990.
5. G Beltram, *Testing the Safety Net,* Bedford Square Press, 1984.

1. POVERTY AND CREDIT

Poverty

Recent trends

In Great Britain in 1987, 10.2 million people were living in poverty (measured as on or below the supplementary benefit (SB) level). A further 5.1 million people had incomes close to this poverty line (between 101 and 140 per cent of SB). In total, 28 per cent of the population were living in or on the margins of poverty. The comparable figure for 1979 was 22 per cent. Using an alternative measure of poverty (on or below 50 per cent of average earnings after housing costs), the picture is remarkably similar. In 1987, 10.5 million people were living in poverty with a further 5.6 million on the margins of poverty (measured as between 51 and 60 per cent of average earnings after housing costs). Compared to the 16.1 million in 1987, 10.1 million people were living in poverty in 1979.[1] Since 1987 (the latest date for which figures are available), there is little to indicate any reduction in the numbers in poverty, and unemployment – one of the major causes of poverty – is on the rise once again.

Those in or on the margins of poverty are largely pensioners, single parents, unemployed, sick and disabled people, and those in low-paid jobs. Between 1979 and 1987, the major change was the growth in the percentage of the poor who were unemployed. The number of pensioners in poverty fell slightly, but as a percentage of those in poverty they fell substantially.[2]

Several factors contribute to the recent growth in the numbers in poverty – unemployment (particularly in the early and mid-1980s); the growth of low-paid, less secure work; and the reduction in some welfare benefits (both their level and scope). Each of these three factors is considered below.

Unemployment

Unemployment rose dramatically after 1979, the numbers increasing from 1,089,000 (4 per cent) to 3,115,000 (11 per cent) between April 1979 and April 1986. The numbers peaked in 1986 at over 3 million, fell to under 2 million late in 1989, but are once again rising. By February 1991 there were 1.8 million 'officially' unemployed – 6.6 per cent. As measured by the official statistics, the changes reflect the variability of the labour market, but also modifications to the 'official' method of calculating the numbers unemployed, changes which have repeatedly sought to exclude a growing number of people who are in fact seeking work. Alternative figures from the Unemployment Unit which include many of those excluded from official statistics suggest that the unemployment rate in June 1990 was 8.5 per cent, representing 2,535,700 individuals.[3]

The distribution of unemployment is unequal geographically, by industry and in terms of its impact on particular groups. Young adults, those over fifty, women and members of ethnic minority groups experience higher than average rates of unemployment. Young adults now constitute over 30 per cent of total unemployment; the growth of unemployment amongst women has been faster than amongst men; older workers are particularly likely to experience long-term unemployment (ie, unemployment of twelve months or longer). In January 1989, nearly 47 per cent of unemployed people over the age of fifty-five had been out of work for more than two years compared with 22 per cent of the unemployed between the ages of twenty-five and forty. Unemployment amongst non-white workers is significantly higher than amongst white workers. In early 1989, the rate of unemployment amongst workers of West Indian origin was nearly double that of whites; amongst Pakistani and Bangladeshi workers it was almost three times as high. Unskilled manual and low-grade clerical workers have higher rates of unemployment than professional and managerial workers.[4]

In addition to the officially unemployed, and the hidden, or unrecorded unemployed, there is also a degree of under-employment, situations in which people are unable to work as many hours as they wish. According to the 1987 *Labour Force*

Survey, half a million workers in part-time jobs were looking for full-time work.

Low-paid employment

Low pay is defined by the Low Pay Unit as two-thirds of median male earnings, excluding overtime pay. For the most recent figures (1989), earnings of £157 gross per week or less constitute low pay, and there are close to 6 million full-time low-paid workers. The extent of full-time low-paid work has been increasing in the 1980s, from 3.5 million in 1982 to 5.6 million in 1988, and by a further 150,000 in 1989. With regard to part-time work, there are around 4 million workers who earn less than the hourly pro rata rate. Low pay particularly affects women, who constitute two-thirds of all low-paid workers.[5]

Several factors account for the increase in the number of workers receiving low pay. For example, government intervention has removed the regulation and protection of young people's wages, and reduced the number of wages inspectors, whose job is to prevent under-payment in already low-paid sectors of employment. Competitive tendering and the pressure to privatise public sector services have sometimes resulted in low-waged work being replaced with even lower-waged work.

Other labour market changes are also contributing to the extent of low pay. One recent development is the growth in the range of forms of employment – such as self-employment, home-working, casual and contract working; a second is the growth in temporary work, and a third, the increase in part-time work. The boundaries of some of these categories are still debated, and the categories can overlap (for example, part-time casual work, temporary casual work), but the direction and scope of change can be identified.

Temporary workers have increased from 621,000 in 1981 to 1,314,000 in 1985. There are approximately 1.8 million home-based workers. Self-employment grew by 442,000 between 1979 and 1984, and nearly 33 per cent of all vacancies in 1988 were for part-time work. These changes are often referred to collectively as part of the 'restructuring' of the labour market that has given rise to a 'flexible' workforce, now thought to encompass a third of the total labour force.[6] Such developments carry a number of implications in terms of financial rewards and security. Many of the jobs are identified as 'bad jobs', in the sense that they are poorly paid and insecure, giving rise to a pattern of intermittent employment.[7] Many such jobs offer few, if any, of the conventional employment protections associated with full-time permanent employee status (eg, insurance, redundancy, sickness and holiday payments), and increasingly such costs are transferred from employer to worker, many of whom are too poorly paid to be able to make the necessary provision. Even where part-time workers are direct employees, their hours of work may be below the qualifying threshold for many forms of employment protection.

The reasons for such a 'restructuring' of the labour market are actively debated, but what is clear is that the labour market exhibits a polarisation between well-paid, secure jobs and poorly-paid, less secure jobs, and that this polarisation is creating a larger pool of low-paid workers.

Welfare benefit – an inadequate resource

The 1980s was a period of substantial change with regard to benefits, increasingly characterised by a shift from benefit as a right towards a means-tested system. In a number of cases, benefits as a right (for example, unemployment benefit or child benefit) have been curtailed (in terms of value and/or eligibility) and this process has particularly affected those who are unemployed. As a result, in 1989/90 almost 75 per cent of unemployed people relied solely on means-tested income support.[8]

The 1986 Social Security Act introduced a fundamental set of changes which aimed to address the streamlining and targeting of benefits.[9] The substance of these changes is not discussed here (see Chapter 2 for a consideration of the social fund), but many of the implications have a significant impact on the issues of borrowing and paying that are the focus of this book. For example, one important consequence is the reduction in resources available to some groups.

Prior to the implementation of the 1986 Act, there were several

TABLE 1
The impact of the 1986 Social Security Act upon Income Support claimants in Social Fund Project authorities

		Losers		Gainers	
Authority	Population[1]	No.[2]	£[3]	No.[4]	£[5]
Barnet	290100	9849	41965	3723	10434
Bedfordshire	502100	15643	67538	5249	14989
Bromley	294500	8693	37471	3225	9085
Buckinghamshire	562200	14242	61703	5138	14682
Cambridgeshire	569800	18143	78159	6366	17575
Cheshire	921600	35367	153909	11343	31236
Derbyshire	901300	38731	164820	12579	33718
Dorset	578900	22836	94725	8980	23158
Fife	325000	16197	69784	4934	13391
Grampian	462800	18430	78813	6366	17080
Gwynedd	222200	11188	47308	3863	10215
Hampshire	1442500	47640	205228	17094	47466
Hertfordshire	950700	24685	106445	9126	25657
Hillingdon	226200	6749	28874	2482	6926
Humberside	843200	40076	174024	12598	34791
Kensington and Chelsea	125800	6560	26061	2740	8189
Leicestershire	835600	29537	126405	10239	28260
Lincolnshire	542900	21432	91151	7102	18994
Nottinghamshire	1006400	45324	193920	14509	40598
North Yorkshire	653400	23587	100062	8584	22677
Oldham	219400	10211	44406	3430	9635
Rochdale	206300	9772	42374	3253	9312
Sefton	298200	14640	63085	4728	12885
Shropshire	370300	14435	61423	4798	13119
Sutton	167500	5251	22282	2066	5659
Wandsworth	252200	13452	57977	5079	15105
Warwickshire	469800	15778	67743	5416	14973
TOTAL	14240900	538448	2307655	185010	509809

NOTES
(1) Local authority population, based upon 1981 Census.
(2) Total number of unemployed, single parent and pensioner income support claimants, by authority, losing benefit.
(3) Total financial loss, by authority, per week.
(4) Total number of unemployed, single parent and pensioner income support claimants, by authority, gaining benefit.
(5) Total financial gain, by authority, per week.

SOURCE: Becker and Silburn (1990)

estimates of the extent to which there would be 'winners' and 'losers' and which groups were likely to be most disadvantaged, although these estimates were not always derived in the same way. Figures provided by the (then) Department of Health and Social Security indicated that approximately a third of supplementary benefit claimants would be adversely affected while just under a half would gain. Other estimates suggested a higher percentage of losers.[10]

Following the implementation of the Act, a number of groups have been monitoring its impact. For example, the Benefits Research Unit has provided data on the winners and losers in twenty-seven local authority areas.[11] The Unit's figures show that, in total, over 2.25 million people were living on or below the income support level. Table 1 shows that while the impact of the changes was 'neutral' for a proportion of people, in 74 per cent of cases where change occurred there was a loss.

TABLE 2
A comparison of claimants' income with average weekly expenditure for all households

	Weekly income support rate (after housing costs) 1990/91	Average weekly expenditure for all households (excl net weekly housing costs) 1989
Single person under 25	£28.80	£120.81 (man) £102.94 (woman)[1]
Single person over 25 (non-pensioner)	£35.70	£120.81 (man) £102.94 (woman)[1]
Couple	£57.60	£163.56
Couple with 2 children under 11	£82.30	£187.06

1. FES does not provide separate expenditure figures for those above and below the age of 25. The figures given relate to all non-retired single people

SOURCE: National Welfare Benefits Handbook, 1990/91, and Family Expenditure Survey, 1989

In addition to the reductions in benefit experienced by some people, there has also been a series of expenditure rises, many of which have increased the hardship of those living in or on the margins of poverty. In particular, the introduction of the poll tax[12] and the higher rate of inflation in the low-paid price index than the ordinary rise in inflation[13] contribute to a situation where benefits are increasingly inadequate. Some indication of this inadequacy is shown in Table 2 which compares the level of resources available to claimants with the average weekly expenditure for all households.

The benefit figures relate to 1990/91 and the expenditure figures to 1989 (the latest figures available from the *Family Expenditure Survey*). The lag in the expenditure figures results in an account of the inadequacy of income support that is in all probability an understatement. It is this gap – between resources and expenditure requirements – and the implication of unmet need, that are closely associated with the growing use of credit amongst low-income households, particularly those with children.

The persistence of need

Those living in poverty have very little money available to them and in many cases cannot meet their basic needs. Evidence of the extent and form of unmet need (defined in a number of different ways) has been provided by many studies over the years and appears to be as prevalent at the start of the 1990s as a decade earlier.

For example, Berthoud, in 1982, showed that amongst families with children, over a third lacked a warm coat and 50 per cent had no change of shoes.[14] In 1985, Mack and Lansley estimated that 7.5 million people lacked at least three of nine items commonly regarded as necessities.[15] More recent evidence of continuing need as a result of routine poverty is available. For example, a survey of sixty-three claimants attending the advice desks of the Welfare Rights Unit in Leicester in 1988 reported that fifty-three had needs such that 'even the most basic and essential items are beyond the reach of those on benefit'.[16] Thirty-one required furniture, thirty household equipment (cookers, fridges, etc) and forty clothes. In almost half of these cases claimants indicated the need existed because they 'just [couldn't] afford it'. Over a quarter could not afford the items because of unpaid bills or debts. A second study concerned with claimants in Northern Ireland showed even higher levels of need (perhaps reflecting the higher costs associated with fuel, and the lower resource base of many Northern Ireland claimants), and in particular that individuals often face several needs at once as the following quotations show:

> Mr C is disabled, married with one child who is a bed wetter. He needs clothing and the bedding has worn out as a result of frequent washing. The cooker has been broken some time.

> Mrs B is a single parent in her mid-fifties. She has lost weight as a result of poor health and also needs bedding. The mattress is worn out and she can't afford to replace it.[17]

Faced with income too low to meet basic needs, people have few options. Effectively, these are to rely on friends and relatives for informal help; to do without; or to take a formal loan from a creditor. Informal help is widespread and takes many forms – basic goods are lent, shared or given and money is borrowed or given.[18] However, this informal support may not be predictable or adequate and may also have problematic implications for personal and social relationships (see page 65). There are also instances where those living in poverty forego basic requirements such as heating or an adequate diet,[19] although this response should be unacceptable in an advanced industrial society. The third response to unmet need - to borrow formally from creditors – has always been an option open to those living in poverty. In the nineteenth and early twentieth century, low-income households used the pawnbroker, tallyman, check traders, money lenders and (later) hire purchase. (The different forms of credit are defined in the Glossary on page 105.) This tradition of credit use has continued throughout the present century, although some aspects of its form may have changed. In the recent past, the growing number of low-income households and the deterioration in the financial resources available to many of them have caused an even greater emphasis and growing reliance on credit use. Evidence of the growth of credit in general and its use amongst those currently in or on the margins of poverty is considered below.

Credit – general trends

During 1989, 75 per cent of households in Britain had access to some form of credit facilities (excluding mortgages). More than 40 million commitments were in force.[20] The growth in credit was marked during the 1980s, as can be seen from Table 3. In real terms, outstanding consumer credit grew by 225 per cent between 1980 and 1988. Consumer expenditure grew by approximately 25 per cent over the same period.[21]

TABLE 3
Credit growth 1980-1988[1]

	£m outstanding		
Date	Personal consumer credit (bank loans, credit cards, retail and finance house credit)	Mortgage credit	Total consumer credit
1980	13,047	52,424	65,471
1982	16,030	76,197	92,227
1983	18,932	90,722	109,654
1984	22,348	108,564	130,909
1985	26,160	127,720	153,880
1986	30,685	153,660	184,375
1987	36,000	184,106	220,106
1988	42,500	224,937	267,437
1989	48,200	255,811	304,011

1. This table excludes informal credit: loans between kin and friends, and from employers.

SOURCE: Financial Statistics 1981-1989

Although there was an increase in both consumer and mortgage credit in this period, around 80 per cent of outstanding credit is associated with borrowing for housing. It is here that the most substantial growth has occurred. Currently, there are approximately 9.3 million mortgagors[22] and Table 4 shows the growth in mortgage lending and the way the mortgage market is shared between a number of mortgage lenders.

The growth in credit during the 1980s involved some new

TABLE 4

Outstanding loans to mortgage lenders, 1973-1988

Lenders	£m						
	1973	1979	1981	1986	1987	1988	1989
Building Societies	14,624	36,986	49,039	116,469	132,238	157,065	152,529
Local Authorities	1,696	3,193	3,917	3,186	2,681	2,428	2,166
Insurance Companies and Pension Funds	1,317	1,854	2,205	3,014	3,904	4,698	4,819
Monetary Sector	1,160	2,403	5,444	25,777	35,836	46,731	79,036
Miscellaneous Financial Institutions				3,515	7,467	12,023	15,087
Other Public Sector	159	572	1,226	1,709	1,808	1,961	2,174
Total	18,956	45,001	62,060	153,660	183,934	224,906	255,811

SOURCE: BSA Bulletin, and Financial Statistics 1974-1989

TABLE 5

The percentage of households in twelve income groups making credit repayments of £25 a week or more, 1982-1986

	1982 %	1984 %	1986 %
All households	3.3	5.9	9.4
Income group:			
£80 to £99	0.4	0.2	–
£100 to £124	0.8	1.6	2.1
£125 to £149	0.7	1.2	3.3
£150 to £174	2.6	3.6	6.1
£175 to £199	2.9	4.8	4.2
£200 to £224	2.0	7.1	4.8
£225 to £249	5.0	5.4	9.9
£250 to £299	7.9	7.8	11.8
£300 to £349	8.1	13.0	16.0
£350 to £399	10.5	18.2	19.6
£400 to £499	18.3	21.4	27.3
£500 or more	13.3	23.1	27.9

NOTE: Because of processing differences, the figures for 1982 are not strictly comparable with those for other years.

SOURCE: OFT (1989)

credit users entering the market, while, in addition, existing credit users extended their commitments. For example, a 1979 survey showed that around 50 per cent of all households had used credit at some point in the previous year.[23] As noted above, by 1989 this figure had risen to 75 per cent. The growth in the percentage of consumer expenditure financed by credit (from approximately 10 per cent in 1980 to nearer 30 per cent today) has resulted in growing repayments for many households. An analysis of data from the *Family Expenditure Surveys* for 1983-1986 shows that average credit repayments rose in every income band; these

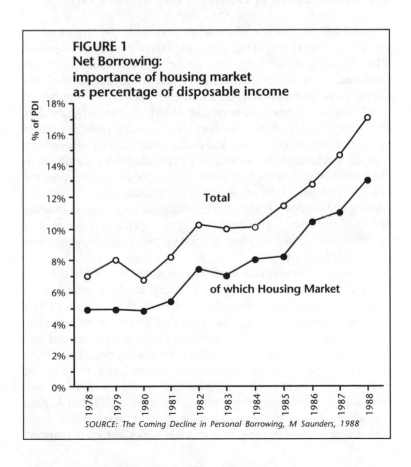

FIGURE 1
Net Borrowing:
importance of housing market
as percentage of disposable income

SOURCE: *The Coming Decline in Personal Borrowing, M Saunders, 1988*

increases constitute a rise in real terms.[24] This same analysis also showed that between 1982 and 1986 the proportion of households making repayments (on both consumer goods and housing) of at least £25 a week had increased in all but one income band (see Table 5).

In total, net personal-sector borrowing (consumer and housing credit) grew from around 7 per cent of personal disposable income in 1978 to 17 per cent in 1988. That overall trend, and within it the significance of housing credit, are shown in Figure 1.

The acceleration of credit growth in the 1980s

The availability and use of credit grew steadily over much of the twentieth century but in the 1980s the rate of growth accelerated. This expansion of personal credit is the result of many interconnecting factors, which have had an impact on both the supply and demand side of the credit market. A number of government policies have been particularly important, including deregulation of the financial markets, a housing policy designed to extend owner occupation and policies that directly incorporate a credit mechanism (for example, a loan scheme for claimants or the establishment of student loans). These policies draw upon and reflect a number of the ideas that are sometimes referred to as the ideology of the New Right – for example, an emphasis on limiting welfare provision, on encouraging individual provision and responsibility, and a concern to 'free-up' markets, allowing them to work 'efficiently'.[25]

Important changes introduced by the government and directed towards the deregulation of the financial markets included the abolition of the bank 'corset' in 1980 and the removal of hire purchase control in 1982. As these restrictions were removed, unsecured consumer lending grew as creditors encouraged and responded to the demand from borrowers who, once freed from the need to provide a deposit, were keen and able to enter the market. The banks also entered the mortgage market and increasingly challenged the building societies (see Table 4, page 16). Given the problematic nature of much of their lending to the Third World and domestic industry, the banks' ability to compete more effectively in the consumer and mortgage markets was crucial to their economic health and development.

The immediate response from the building societies was to meet the competition by dismantling their interest rate cartel. As a result, the mortgage market grew increasingly competitive. These policies effectively brought to an end mortgage queues and rationing and clearly satisfied considerable pent-up demand. However, the amount of credit available, coupled with the restriction of building society lending to the mortgage market, resulted in a search for additional mortgage borrowers. These could only come from an extension of mortgage lending 'down market'. In general, the amount that people could borrow in relation to their income increased, while the percentage deposit required often decreased. Building societies also pressed the government for further deregulation to enable them to compete in the non-mortgage market,[26] and this was achieved with the passing of the Building Societies Act 1986.

The commitment by the 1979 Thatcher government to extend owner occupation – particularly through the 'right to buy' legislation – added a further impetus to the credit market. During the 1980s, more than a million local authority houses and new town development corporation houses were sold in the United Kingdom and the building societies were able to respond to this demand. Each sale involved a credit agreement. Each mortgage provided an opportunity and security for further borrowing should the household so decide.

The high rates of inflation in the late 1970s and early 1980s also encouraged borrowers to view their credit commitments as economically rational. Rising house prices, and the growing equity available to borrowers, increased consumer confidence and encouraged further borrowing, often via the mechanism of equity withdrawal.[27]

These general developments are part of the context within which particular groups of people use credit (their income, age and household structure are other important factors). As has already been noted, not everyone uses credit to the same extent and it is therefore important to consider explanations for the actual take-up and extent of credit use.

Frequently a framework which contrasts income and

expenditure over the lifecycle is adopted.[28] Typically, income is low when households are first formed or have their children, although subsequently income rises. In contrast, expenditure needs may be substantial and pressing in the early years of a household's life (for example, for housing, furniture, electrical goods, and the costs associated with young children), and lower in later life. Younger households – and those with young children – may smooth the imbalance between income and expenditure needs by borrowing now against future income. Poorer households (especially if their lack of resources is acute rather than chronic) may borrow against better times. Within this framework, younger households are likely to be substantial users of credit, and the use of credit by those with limited resources is not unexpected. Alternative views on credit take-up give greater stress to the impact of rising income on the demand for credit,[29] or to the impact of cultural influences.[30] There are also influences from the credit market which contribute to credit use. For example, some commentators stress that the easy availability of credit, coupled with aggressive advertising, 'creates' a demand, and encourages people to take on commitments to a greater extent than they might if left to their own devices, and certainly past the point that is prudent. This danger is exacerbated where potential borrowers lack any real knowledge about the costs and conditions of credit. Fears of this kind have been expressed in the 1980s following the processes outlined earlier that created a deregulated and more competitive market.

The influences on credit take-up have been discussed as though they acted independently of each other. In practice, of course, they interact. For example, within the lifecycle framework the size of current income is an important constraint. Individuals from different cultural backgrounds may have differing views on credit that affect the extent of take-up. Equally, the pressures and inducements of the market are likely to have some effect on us all, although to differing degrees.

Clearly, much of the expansion in credit in the 1980s has been closely tied to credit 'for improvement' based on rising incomes, rising expectations and increased security. Many people have been able to make choices about what to buy and how to finance purchases as the financial markets have offered more forms of, and easy access to, credit. However, not everyone has shared in these developments to the same extent, and some not at all. Rising average incomes and accelerating credit mask continuing and growing inequalities with regard to both income and access to credit. One consequence is that the long-established use of credit by those with low incomes, in order to manage their poverty, has not only continued, but in all probability grown, as the numbers of poor and near-poor households have grown and their relative disadvantage increased.

Credit and low income

The most recent evidence concerning credit comes from a survey conducted in 1989 by the Policy Studies Institute (PSI). Earlier studies, conducted in 1987 by Public Attitude Surveys for the Office of Fair Trading (referred to here as the PAS study) and in 1979 by the National Consumer Council (NCC), can be used to consider the extent of changes in credit use over the 1980s. Although both surveys provide a great deal of information on credit use in general, it is only the findings regarding low-income credit use which are considered here. Table 6 presents some results from the PSI survey and indicates that, as household income increases, so do the numbers using credit, along with the number of commitments held.

It is clear that low-income households are relatively less likely to use credit than more affluent households; they are also likely to have approximately half the number of commitments of the highest income group. The pattern of use is also affected by age and household composition. Pensioners make little use of credit and families with children greater use.

Some assessment of the growth in the number of credit users over the 1980s can be obtained by comparing the results of the PSI survey with earlier surveys. Table 7 sets out some of the relevant data. In drawing any conclusions, particular attention should be paid to the footnotes that indicate important differences between the surveys. The commentary underneath assesses the likely impact of these differences. All things considered, however, the figures suggest an increase in the number of low-income households

TABLE 6
Extent of credit use by income group[1] (non-pensioner households)

Net weekly income	Percentage using any credit	Mean no. of commitments for those using credit
Up to £100	69	2.09
£100 to £150	77	2.37
£150 to £200	84	2.58
£200 to £250	82	2.82
£250 to £300	88	3.04
£300 to £400	96	3.35
£400 or more	96	4.07
Average	86	3.02

1. Mortgage credit is excluded. Both commercial and non-commercial consumer credit are included (eg, overdraft, store cards, social fund loans, loans from kin).
SOURCE: R Berthoud and E Kempson (1990), Credit and Debt in Britain: First Findings.

using credit, both when the start and the end of the decade are compared, but also when 1990 is compared to 1987.

As already noted, the resources available to many low-income households have often remained static or suffered a relative decline over the same period. Thus, even if expenditure needs and costs had remained the same, in many instances budgeting pressures would have grown. In practice, over the period in question many expenses have risen, potentially drawing in more credit users. In addition, credit use has been encouraged as some claimants have been steered or pushed towards the social fund or other creditors following the abolition of single payments in 1988.[31]

Another low-income, non-claimant group that has been drawn into credit use to a considerable extent in the 1980s is students. Their financial resources have declined (the value of the student grant has dropped by more than 35 per cent since 1962, while other costs central to them have risen; more than a third of parents are not meeting the expected parental contribution; access to benefits is curtailed or denied) and in addition they now have to meet costs such as the poll tax. As a result of these pressures, many

---

TABLE 7
Credit use by lowest income group: 1980, 1987, 1990

Date	% of lowest income group using credit	weekly income of lowest income group
1980	22	£40 or under
1987	45	£100 or under (gross)
1990	69	£100 or under (net)

SOURCES: Derived from NCC (1980) Consumer and Credit; PAS (1987) Consumers' Use of Credit Survey; PSI (1990) Credit and Debt in Britain: First Findings

There are a number of differences between these surveys that are important here:

1. PAS (1987) records gross income, PSI (1990) net income.
2. NCC (1980) and PAS (1987) include pensioners, PSI does not.
3. PAS (1987) and NCC (1980) treat mortgages as credit commitments, PSI categorises them as a household expense.
4. NCC and PAS report credit use in the recent past, PSI reports available credit facilities in the last 12 months.
5. PAS consider debts over the last five years, PSI over the last year.
6. PAS define 'debt' as 'difficulties' with payments (non-payment, part-payment, but also a struggle to find the money). PSI focuses more explicitly on non-payment.

It is important to consider the likely impact of points 1-6 on the increase in low-income credit use shown in Table 7. For example, at these income levels gross and net payments are close, and the different measures used have little impact. The inclusion of pensioners (PAS) is likely to boost the recording of non-use, exaggerating the comparisons with the non-pensioner survey. Conversely, NCC and PAS include mortgage commitments, increasing the recording of credit use. This effect probably outweighs that of the pensioner/non-pensioner comparison. 'Recent' credit use (PAS) is likely to approximate to 'available credit facilities over the last 12 months' (PSI) in so far as low-income households use less commercial credit and find access more difficult than higher income households, and would be unlikely to seek credit without the intention to use it.

---

students have borrowed from commercial creditors (PAS indicated that just under 50 per cent of students had borrowed, particularly from the banks). The government has now frozen the level of the student grant and from October 1990 instituted a 'complementary' loan system. Although at the time of writing take-up of these loans appears to be less than was expected, there is little doubt that the number of students borrowing money (both under the loan scheme and from commercial sources) for day-to-day living expenses is growing. Their current resources preclude repayment while they remain students. As a result, at the point where they might usually look to credit to help establish themselves as an independent household they may already be indebted.[32]

Low-income households which use credit have also been using more of it (as has every other group). For example, households with an income of £80-£100 in 1982 had average credit payments of £6.90 per week. The comparable income group in 1986 had average payments of £9.70 per week. 'The credit repayments in many instances have increased by a greater percentage than the probable income increases.'[33] Those households with weekly incomes between £125 and £175 had the heaviest commitments in relation to income. Households within this income group might then be amongst the most vulnerable to repayment difficulties.

There is also evidence that the increase in low-income credit use is not necessarily a matter of choice. The 1987 PAS survey showed low-income respondents citing 'necessity' as the reason for credit use to a much greater extent than those with higher incomes who stressed 'convenience'. Overall, 36 per cent of respondents used credit out of necessity, but the figure was higher (45 per cent) amongst those with weekly incomes between £50 and £100. The unemployed indicated 'necessity' to an even greater extent – 52 per cent of those unemployed for less than six months and 64 per cent of those unemployed for more than six months gave this as the principal reason for credit use.

Evidence from studies of low-income households

Further evidence of the continuing and growing use of credit and its relationship to need comes from specific studies of low-income households. A study by Berthoud in 1982 showed that 40 per cent of claimants had credit commitments and average repayments of £4.70 per week. Agreements existed with mail order companies (21 per cent), on hire purchase (13 per cent), and for loans (6 per cent), while 15 per cent had other forms of credit. The heaviest use was amongst claimant couples with children who averaged £6.60 a week on credit agreements.[34] The picture was little changed in 1987 when a survey of claimants in Oxford again showed the significance of credit, particularly in the lives of households with children, with 71 per cent of couples with children and 75 per cent of lone parents using credit.[35] Additional evidence is also available from research into some aspects of the social fund (one part being a system of loans that replaced most single payments to claimants in 1988). By 1989, 352,048 claimants were making repayments on social fund loans and £112 million had been provided as credit to those on income support.[36] In particular, reports from many parts of the country reveal the extent to which many claimants are overburdened with credit, with multiple commitments such as mail order agreements, trading checks, provident loans and hire purchase, all forming part of their routine existence.[37] Sixty-four out of sixty-seven families interviewed by Bradshaw and Holmes during their study of claimant households with children on Tyneside had commitments on loans averaging £441, with average weekly repayments around £10.35 (11 per cent of income).[38]

It is clear that day-to-day living necessitates credit use by those on low incomes, but social and ritual occasions are also important triggers. Birthdays and Christmas not only pose additional financial burdens, but within families also precipitate added anxieties about being a 'good parent' or about 'disappointing the kids', which in turn can result in a pressure to use additional credit.

> The only way the children will get the present they want will be to get it from a club which will mean more debt, that will cripple [me] more.

> We rely on catalogues where we can buy over 50-week terms, and have just paid off the debt when Christmas is here again and you have to start all over again.[39]

A similar use of credit (and subsequent debt) for both economic and symbolic reasons can be seen amongst low-income young adults, particularly those under twenty-five who are in low-income employment, only eligible for a lower rate of income support or, for various reasons, excluded from benefit altogether.[40] Often credit is the only way in which these young adults can buy basic items such as clothes.[41] Adulthood is also about independence and reciprocal relationships, and for many the giving as well as receiving of presents is an important component. Faced with no income or low wages that preclude saving or discretionary income, young people often decide that credit provides a means to participate in an adult world.

So far, the focus has been on consumer needs – clothing, furniture and food; and credit use – hire purchase, mail order, social fund loans, etc. Credit is also taken for housing and this is considered next.

Low-income owner occupation

The expansion of mortgage lending accounts for most of the growth in outstanding credit in the 1980s. Until the late 1970s, home ownership was largely the preserve of the secure professional white-collar employee, and skilled craftsworker. In 1979, there were approximately 6 million mortgage loans held. In 1990, there were 9.3 million mortgage loans in force.[42] This expansion is the outcome of several factors, including the increase in the number of households (particularly single person households); the impact of the right to buy legislation (with discounted prices and supportive financial arrangements); the decline in the quantity and quality of local authority rental property (with associated lengthening waiting lists); the move towards market rents; the deregulation of financial processes and increasingly competitive markets; and the clear desire of many people to own a property. In the 1980s, the number of home owners grew principally by mortgage institutions extending their down-market lending, drawing in a greater number of first-time low-income borrowers. For example, between 1982 and 1986, amongst all households headed by a manual worker, the percentage with mortgages grew from 42.9 per cent to 52.6 per cent (exceeding the growth amongst non-manual households).[43] Within that group, the percentage of semi-skilled mortgagors increased from 24 to 34 per cent between 1982 and 1985. Most were in employment when they entered the tenure.

First-time buyers tend to put down smaller deposits and take higher percentage loans than subsequent movers. Where they are also low-income borrowers they are even less likely to have savings and are often looking for the highest possible percentage advance. In 1980, 34 per cent of first-time building society borrowers had 100 per cent loans, in each of 1988 and 1989, 24 and 36 per cent. In many areas, the rise in house prices has also stretched the loan-to-income ratio. The percentage of borrowers taking a loan from a building society of three or more times the size of their income grew from 4 per cent in 1985 to 12 per cent in 1988,[44] although this is not solely a low-income phenomenon. However, those who are poor, principally through low pay, have increasingly become home owners, and have often taken on heavy commitments relative to income in order to do so. According to the Office of Fair Trading:

> The percentage of households whose mortgage commitments could be regarded as heavy in relation to their income rose from 0.9 per cent to 1.4 per cent between 1982 and 1986. The latter figure represents a figure in excess of a quarter of a million households in the United Kingdom. Households with incomes between £80-£149 a week appear most likely to have heavy commitments: about 4 per cent did so in 1986, the figure having risen from about 2 per cent in 1982.[45]

Sometimes low-income borrowers have bought poor quality property that requires maintenance or improvement, and a considerable number have borrowed again to effect the improvements, taking a loan either from their original mortgagee, or from a bank or finance house, and secured the loan against their property. In 1986, there were a million secured loans in force, 75 per cent taken for home improvements and repairs.[46]

Low-paid mortgagors are not necessarily the poorest section of the poor, but in many cases they do have household earnings that are below the low-pay threshold as defined by the Low Pay Unit, or the Council of Europe. Their budgets have often been stretched by the first mortgage, and in addition, in the mid- and late-1980s, they faced many unavoidable increases in costs (rates, poll tax, increasing interest rates), and often pressures to take on additional loans.

Creating credit

Studies of low-income budgeting patterns have long made clear the way in which the 'juggling' of payments is central to financial management. Household members often face the task of 'robbing Peter to pay Paul'. Frequently, a line of credit is created from within the household budget by delaying payment on a due bill and releasing the money for something else more pressing. This credit is 'interest free' and sometimes referred to as 'proxy' credit.[47] The delay in payment has, however, to be tightly monitored and managed in order to prevent a 'real' default occurring. 'Proxy' credit via rent, fuel and other service payment is probably widespread, but other examples can also be found. One such example is provided by a recent study of mail order agents, the majority of whom were living on benefit. These agents took orders for products from their customers who paid for them when the goods were delivered to them. Depending on how quickly they worked at the deliveries, agents often had a few days between collecting in the money and the deadline for transmitting it to the mail order company. In the meantime, this money was often 'borrowed' for food, or a pressing bill, almost always with the intention of repaying it out of the next benefit payment. In a majority of cases, repayment of the proxy credit had not been possible. These indebted agents then lost their jobs and additional income, as well as being subject to debt collection processes by the mail order company.[48]

This chapter has reviewed some of the evidence concerning credit use amongst those living in or on the margins of poverty, suggesting that credit use arises from the gap between income and need that exists in many households. Credit is still used less by poor families than by more affluent families. Fewer of them use credit, and when it is used, the commitments are smaller, although both the number of low-income credit users and the extent of credit commitments have grown over the 1980s. Many of the low-paid poor have been drawn into owner occupation and it is here that some of the heaviest credit commitments in relation to income are found. However, with the exception of mortgages, little has been said about the types of credit used by poorer households. Questions of equality of access and costs have not been considered either, and the next chapter takes up these issues.

NOTES
1. C Oppenheim, *Poverty: The Facts*, CPAG Ltd, 1990.
2. *See* note 1.
3. *Creative Accounting*, Unemployment Unit, 1990.
4. *See* note 1.
5. *Low Pay in Great Britain and the Regions*, Low Pay Unit Parliamentary Briefing No 1, 1990.
6. C Hakim, 'Homeworking in Britain' in R Pahl, *On Work: Historical, Comparative and Theoretical Approaches*, Basil Blackwell, 1988.
7. C Harris, *Redundancy and Recession*, Basil Blackwell, 1987.
8. *See* note 1.
9. A Dilnot and S Webb, 'The Social Security Reforms', in A Dilnot and A Walker (eds), *The Economics of Social Security*, OUP, 1989.
10. CPAG, *The Social Security Act: A Brief Guide*, CPAG, 1988.
11. S Becker and R Silburn, *The New Poor Clients*, Community Care and Benefits Research Unit, 1990.
12. P Esam and C Oppenheim, *A Charge on the Community: the poll tax, benefits and the poor*, CPAG Ltd/LGIU, 1989.
13. K Kiernan and M Wicks, *Family Change and Future Policy*, Family Policy Studies Centre and Joseph Rowntree Memorial Trust, 1990.
14. R Berthoud, *PSI Survey of Supplementary Benefit Claimants*, 1982.
15. J Mack and S Lansley, *Poor Britain*, Allen and Unwin, 1985.
16. S McKenna and J Gurney, *In Hock to the State*, Leicester CPAG, 1988.
17. E Evason, L Allamby and R Woods, *The Deserving and Undeserving Poor*, CPAG (Northern Ireland), 1989.
18. Examples can be found in many studies – for example, L Burghes, *Living from Hand to Mouth*, CPAG, 1980; J Ford, *The Indebted Society*, Routledge, 1988.
19. H Graham, 'Being Poor: Perceptions and Coping Strategies of Lone Mothers', in J Brannen and G Wilson, *Give and Take in Families*, Unwin Hyman, 1987.
20. R Berthoud and E Kempson, *Credit and Debt in Britain: First Findings*, Policy Studies Institute, 1990.
21. *Social Trends 1991*, HMSO, 1991.
22. *House of Commons Hansard*, 28 March 1990, col 196.
23. National Consumer Council, *Consumers and Credit*, NCC, 1980.
24. Office of Fair Trading, *Overindebtedness*, HMSO, 1989.
25. See, for example, N Barry, *The New Right*, Croom Helm, 1987.
26. There was a series of reports published, including the Stow Report, 1979, and the Spalding Report, 1983, arguing for greater powers.
27. Equity withdrawal refers to the process of releasing capital accumulated as a result of house prices rising.
28. F Modigliani and R Blumberg, 'Utility analysis and the consumption function: an analysis of cross sectional data', in K Kurihara (ed), *Post Keynesian Economics*, 1955.
29. A Hartropp, 'The Determinants of Consumer Borrowing in the UK: 1970-1989', Discussion Paper in Economics, Brunel University, 1990.

30. A Lewis, Transcript of 'File on Four' programme on credit, 1990.

31. R Lister, 'Conclusions: Privatising Need', in G Craig (ed), *Your Flexible Friend,* Social Security Consortium, 1989.

32. Discussion of the likely impact of student loans on future credit use in National Consumer Council, *Credit and Debt: The Consumer Interest,* NCC, 1990.

33. *See* note 24.

34. *See* note 14.

35. M Noble, G Smith, J Payne and J Roberts, *The Other Oxford,* Department of Social and Administrative Studies, University of Oxford, 1987.

36. Quoted in S Becker and R Silburn, *see* note 11.

37. For example, *see* notes 16 and 17.

38. J Bradshaw and H Holmes, *Living on the Edge: a study of the living standards of families on benefits in Tyne and Wear,* Tyneside CPAG, 1989.

39. C Oppenheim and S McEvaddy, *Christmas on the Breadline,* CPAG Ltd, 1987.

40. S McCrae, *Young and Jobless,* Policy Studies Institute, 1987.

41. *See* note 40.

42. *See* note 22.

43. *See* note 24.

44. *Housing Finance Quarterly,* BSA/CLM, April 1990.

45. *See* note 24.

46. National Consumer Council, *Security Risks,* NCC, 1987.

47. This term was used in an NCC publication. *See* note 32.

48. J Ford and J Piper, *Representatives in Debt,* Department of Social Sciences, Loughborough University, 1989.

2. CREDIT – SOURCES, ACCESS AND COST

Patterns of credit use

Currently in Britain there are more than fifteen main forms of credit in use. They range from mortgages, bank loans and credit cards to check trading, tallymen and the social fund (see the Glossary). Most forms of credit can be clearly located in one of four categories:

> **commercial** (legally regulated market transactions – for example, bank loans, store cards or check trading);
> **informal** (non-market, personally based transactions such as a loan from a friend);
> **state credit** (for example, social fund loans); and
> **unregulated, extortionate market transactions** (for example, money-lending as undertaken by loan sharks).

The balance between the different forms of credit is not static and in the course of this century there have been a number of changes in the types of credit available and the patterns of credit use. For example, pawnbroking has declined and hire purchase has recently become relatively less prominent. Bank credit cards (Access and Visa) were unknown in Britain before the mid-1960s, but have grown substantially over the last decade (the number of people using some form of credit card doubling between 1979 and 1987). Store cards, bank and finance house loans, and mortgage credit have grown too, both in terms of value and the numbers of borrowers. Social fund loans were not introduced until 1988. This said, these changes have not fundamentally altered the long-standing position whereby different forms of credit are used by people at different levels of income.[1]

In the early stages of credit expansion in the late nineteenth and early twentieth centuries, the tendency was for different creditors to serve different socio-economic groups – pawnbrokers and check traders for the poor, hire purchase for the growing number of white-collar workers, and bank overdrafts for the professional classes. While there has been a trend towards a less differentiated market (in terms of who uses what), some clear differences remain in the types of credit predominantly used by households with different levels of income. The use of a number of commercial credit sources by income, as reported in 1987, is shown in Figure 2. Low-income households use several forms of credit but clearly mail-order credit is particularly important:

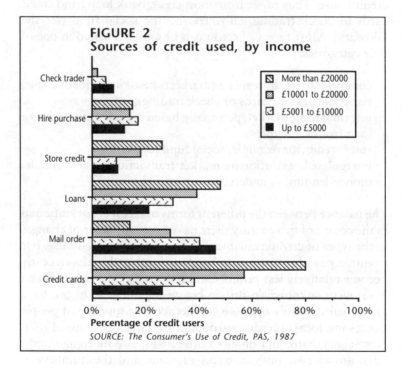

FIGURE 2
Sources of credit used, by income

Check trader
Hire purchase
Store credit
Loans
Mail order
Credit cards

| More than £20000
| £10001 to £20000
| £5001 to £10000
| Up to £5000

0%   20%   40%   60%   80%   100%
Percentage of credit users
SOURCE: *The Consumer's Use of Credit, PAS, 1987*

The 1990 PSI data confirm the continuing relevance of the pattern described above. In addition, informal credit from family and friends is important:

Low-income families, lone parents, council tenants and families where the head of household was not in work, were the groups who were most likely to have borrowed money from relatives and other non-commercial sources. These two sources [mail-order and non-commercial credit] therefore provided a very high proportion of the limited amount of credit used by low-income families.[2]

Research in the early 1980s showed that there were some forms of credit used predominantly or exclusively by those living in or on the margins of poverty – for example, tallymen, money-lenders and check traders. In 1980, the NCC survey showed that 21 per cent of semi- and unskilled manual workers were using or had used check trading, compared to 8 per cent of routine (non-professional/managerial) clerical workers.[3] Research undertaken by Adler and Wozniak in Scotland commented that clubs and check trading were 'an important method of purchase for many low-income households in Central Scotland'.[4] Similarly, Ashley drew attention to the role of money-lenders, check traders, doorstep sales and hire purchase in the lives of the poor.[5] More recent surveys of credit use, however, indicate rather lower levels of use of many of these forms of credit, suggesting a shift in the pattern of credit use by low-income families. For example, the 1987 PAS survey showed only 2 per cent of households overall using check trading within the last five years, and 1 per cent buying from tallymen. In the main, however, users were poor. Three per cent of those earning under £5,000 gross per year, and a similar percentage of those earning £5,000-£10,000, had used check trading. At higher income levels usage fell to 0.3 per cent.[6]

Some commentators, however, have suggested that these results are surprisingly low, not just for check trading but also for other traditional forms of low-income commercial credit, and suggest there may be some under-reporting.[7] It is also likely that the aggregate figures for these particular forms of credit mask some much higher levels of lending to particular groups in some specific locations – for example, on the poorest, stigmatised local authority estates. Data from recent studies of families living in poverty and from the trade associations that represent check traders, money-lenders and other weekly-collect creditors lend credence to the suggestion of an understatement of the extent of use.

In a recent discussion of poverty, Becker noted an area where 'Residents are served by a fleet of mobile food vans, tallymen and fish and chip shops'.[8] An in-depth study of sixty-seven families living on benefit in Tyneside noted that over half had current agreements with the Provident Clothing and Supply Company (check traders) averaging £196. Three had borrowed from money-lenders and one from a pawnbroker.[9] Other studies confirm this general picture.[10] A number of local authority trading standards departments have also noted the prevalence of both legal money-lenders and illegal loan sharks, particularly on poor local authority estates.[11] A recent report says with regard to the Strathclyde region of Scotland:

> Illegal money lending ... flourishes in areas suffering from a high level of general poverty, where they prey on the most financially disadvantaged members of society.[12]

The authors note the way the loan sharks operate openly, typically outside benefit offices, post offices and pubs. In one of the cases documented, an illegal money-lender was found to have sixty-two benefit books in his possession with a face value of £23,000. In another case, a ring of five 'worked' a shopping centre, and when apprehended were estimated to have an annual average income of £98,000. The persistence of loan sharking is clear when the authors comment that as one is prosecuted another takes his place.

Check traders, registered money-lenders, and other self-financed retailers/creditors who collect credit payments from borrowers on a weekly basis are represented by two trade associations – CCA(UK) and the National Consumer Credit Federation (a smaller trade association). One thousand companies (including some in Southern Ireland) belong to CCA(UK). These companies employ 15,000 representatives and have over 4 million customers. They offer credit to the value of £400 million per year, usually sums between £20 and £300, typically over a six-month period. In 1969, the Crowther Committee estimated that there were around 3,300 itinerant credit traders, a figure that CCA(UK) believe was an underestimate. They suggest that currently there are between 6,000 and 7,000 weekly-collect creditors. They have borrowers in all socio-economic groups, but the greatest concentration of borrowers is amongst low-income households.

Neither the qualitative accounts of poor households and poor estates nor the data from CCA(UK) can be regarded as any more than an indication of a higher level of activity by check traders, tallymen, money-lenders, etc, than reported by recent surveys. Firmer evidence of the extent and range of credit transactions amongst some groups and in some areas needs to be sought. One useful way forward would be to develop a 'credit audit' in defined areas and/or groups. This would be a difficult research exercise, but one which would show much, not only about what is used, but how and why; the ways in which various networks of credit relate to each other and the extent to which there are local credit cultures.

Access and the costs of credit

Access 'is not an area in which free choice operates, but is closely determined by income, occupation, tenure, sex, age, home address and culture'.[13] The record of previous credit use may also be important. Because credit is a risk-taking activity, requiring borrowers to sustain payments over a period of time, all creditors (except perhaps those in the informal sector) look for evidence of security and certainty. High-income and high-status occupations are used to signify low risk. Equally, collateral in the form of property may be required, or may simply be used as further evidence of financial stability and financial assets. Many of these criteria have been formalised into credit scoring or credit assessment techniques. Those borrowers who offer the greatest security have access to the widest range of credit, including the cheapest credit. Other borrowers have more limited access, usually only to the more expensive forms of credit. Some may be excluded altogether from credit. Thus, access and costs vary considerably. These dimensions are drawn together in Table 8 which is organised specifically from the perspective of the low-income borrower. Although the costs relate to 1987, the inequalities revealed by the data persist today.

The central position accorded to income, occupation and employment in assessing credit-worthiness results in particular groups finding their access to credit constrained. Those with limited incomes, low-status jobs or no jobs are disadvantaged.

TABLE 8
The cost of credit to low income groups

Sources of consumer credit	Typical APR June 1987	Availability to disadvantaged groups
Credit Unions	12.68%	Availability limited by location

Credit Unions are open to all, subject to the common bond between members. A long-term option as members need to build up some savings before they can borrow.

Banks

Personal loans	19.00%	Not available
Overdrafts	–	Not available

Banks are withdrawing from deprived areas. They are reluctant to open accounts to the 'disadvantaged' but will sometimes open a deposit account for a trial period with the possibility of a current account later.

Building Societies

Mortgages	12.25%	Not available
Personal loans	19.50%	

The disadvantaged are usually tenants and are rejected as not creditworthy by using credit scoring.

Credit cards

Access, Visa	23.10%	Not available
Shop cards eg Marks & Spencer, C&A, etc	29.80%	

Disadvantaged applicants would be rejected as not creditworthy using credit scoring.

Finance companies

Personal loans	Variable	Not available
Hire purchase		
Credit/conditional sale		

Disadvantaged applicants rejected as uncreditworthy.

...continued

Sources of consumer credit	Typical APR June 1987	Availability to disadvantaged groups
Catalogue companies		
eg, Littlewoods, Kays	Not available	Sometimes available
Companies are becoming reluctant to deal with people in deprived areas. There is some black-listing, particularly in areas with a lot of high-rise flats. Limited range of goods.		
Check trading		
eg, Provident	Expensive	Sometimes available
One of the major sources of credit to the disadvantaged but difficulty is being experienced as companies are increasingly asking for guarantors, which creditors cannot get.		
Licensed money-lenders		
Cash loans	300%	Sometimes available
Degree of compliance with law varies between traders. Often require security for larger loans. Some are little better than unlicensed money-lenders.		
Unlicensed money-lenders		
Cash loans or specific goods, eg, shoes, pots and pans, bedding offered for a weekly payment	Over 1,000%	Easy
Loan sharks operating without consumer credit licence – no documentation given, no paying-in books. Total cost of goods may be twice the shop price for equivalent goods. Intimidation and strong-arm tactics used in cases of default.		

SOURCE: Derived from The Fair Trader, Vol 1, No 7, 1987

This group includes many women and members of ethnic minority groups, because of broader social and economic processes that allocate them to low-paid and/or part-time jobs, or high levels of unemployment. In addition, non-economic factors play a part in structuring access to credit. Knowledge of financial processes and financial institutions is unequal, and the rational assumptions about 'shopping around', even amongst limited alternatives, may be relinquished in favour of familiarity and certainty of acceptance.

Traditional patterns of credit use within families and neighbourhoods may be continued from one generation to the next. Creditors often recruit borrowers by direct calling or through word of mouth. Because of the economic and social circumstances of borrowers, many low-income creditors have a quasi-monopolistic position.

A number of the processes discussed above with regard to access are summed up in the following quotation. Although it was written explicitly about pawnbroking in the early twentieth century, it remains relevant to the use of much low-income credit today:

> Not only need for credit but familiarity encouraged many customers to stick with both the pawnbroker and other local traders whose prices were often higher than the cash stores elsewhere, for lack of knowledge and fear of asking are crucial aspects of the credit market. They frequently generate a great deal of anxiety which tends to be resolved through habit or personal recommendation.[14]

Where needs are substantial and urgent, unconstrained access in terms of speed and limited formality is important, and these are reflected in the organisation of creditors such as mail-order or money-lenders. Provided the sum per week seems 'acceptable' to the borrower, wider economic calculations may take a back seat.

Exclusion from credit

Recently, attention has been drawn to the way in which many poorer people are excluded from credit because they do not have a bank account.[15] In 1985, more than 15 million adults were in this position. As can be seen from Table 9, 50 per cent of all households with less than £3,000 per annum and almost 50 per cent of unskilled/semi-skilled workers had no bank connection. By 1989, the number without a bank account had fallen, but still stood at over 11 million.[16] Clearly, this situation may reflect their choice – but it may also reflect the choice of the bank.

TABLE 9
The unbanked

% of adults without a current (cheque-book) account

All adults	31.2	Income group	
All men	27.4	Not stated	59.0
All women	34.6	£2,999 or less	51.3
Social class		£3,000 to £4,999	34.8
AB	11.8	£5,000 to £6,999	25.1
C1	18.2	£7,000 to £8,999	18.5
C2	30.8	£9,000 to £10,999	14.8
D	43.7	£11,000 to £14,999	11.0
E	58.7	£15,000 and over	11.3

SOURCE: Target Group Index BRMB, 1985

Until the mid-1980s, many people were excluded from banking services in a fairly direct way because the banks required deposits and references and imposed charges on those who could not maintain a minimum of £100 in their account. Since 1988, and the introduction of 'free' banking in the UK, those on low incomes have had no material disincentive to open accounts, but there is evidence of discouragement through more indirect and subtle means. Toporowski shows how the increased use of credit scoring by the banks has meant that while those with low scores (typically low-income, rental tenure, 'non-status' customers) may be granted a current account, they may be denied a cheque guarantee card or bank credit card. Thus, the limited possession of credit cards by semi- and unskilled workers in 1980 was little changed in 1987 (6 per cent in 1980 and 10 per cent in 1987) as contrasted with the growth of credit cards amongst skilled manual workers. Ten per cent had Access and Visa cards in 1980, but 32 per cent in 1987.[17] However, it is not only differential access to bank credit that matters. Without a cheque guarantee card the bank account is practically worthless to a customer as cheques cannot be used for shop purchases, nor can cash withdrawals be made from ATM machines or bank branches other than the customer's own.

Exclusion also comes about as a result of changes by the banks in their location policies which have removed or reduced services in many areas of high unemployment. The banks may also 'discourage' as well as exclude. For example, Toporowski discusses the banks' image, suggesting that it appears imposing and unfamiliar to working-class, low-income people who are therefore reluctant to ask about potential services. There is evidence that those who are unfamiliar with banking fear that the officials will be judgmental about their financial organisation or wish to know unduly about their personal lives. The calculation of costs (quarterly, and after transactions) fits uneasily with low-income budgeting patterns that tend to be organised on a weekly basis with known commitments.

Banks also increasingly market and cross-sell their products. In addition, they target existing customers. Existing borrowers often receive advance notice of new products and so indirectly the unbanked have a more restricted set of products from which to choose. Thus, direct and indirect exclusion of the poor from banking has a number of disadvantageous implications, not least exclusion from some of the cheapest forms of credit (see Table 8).

Historically, some banks have been more explicitly linked with low-income groups than others – for example, the Trustee Savings Bank (TSB), National Savings and the National Giro Bank. These relationships may, however, be changing. The TSB has been privatised and the Giro Bank sold to the Alliance and Leicester Building Society. The TSB now has shareholders and city analysts to satisfy via an increasingly commercial operation, and already the process of rationalisation has begun and there has been a withdrawal of services from some inner city areas, just as happened with the clearing banks. National Giro has a traditional customer base of women and low-income savers, but may also be prone to the changes that stem from competitive pressures.

With regard to exclusion, the building societies provide an interesting example. Traditionally, the societies attracted low-income savers, even while, as late as the 1970s, they often adopted exclusionary practices *vis-à-vis* two-person low-income households and single women wishing to take mortgages. However, as the commercial, financial and political environment changed in the early and mid-1980s, not only did the building societies drop many exclusionary practices, they also competed aggressively and courted low-income borrowers. In the late 1980s and early 1990s, building societies are once again more exclusive. They are less and less distinguishable from the banks and are players in an increasingly competitive market, offering secured and unsecured loans with similar commercial concerns and practices as other creditors, including the need to manage and, if possible, avoid default. Credit scoring, credit selling and targeting are important additions to building society practice and are likely to discourage any further extension of facilities to the poor, and potentially limit the facilities with regard to existing low-income borrowers.

Thus, partial or complete exclusion from banking services, because the banks and building societies control a substantial amount of lower-cost credit, is clearly disadvantageous for poorer people. However, exclusion in one area does not suppress demand, but channels low-income borrowers towards other creditors, who, while also adopting credit scoring policies, may set the entry criteria differently, and reflect this in the price.

Lenders to low-income borrowers

In contrast to the exclusion process, some forms of credit are directly available to the poor, and often targeted on them. They are, however, expensive. The credit is often presented in terms of the criteria known to be important to those who have to budget on low incomes – weekly payments are low, collection is direct and personal, and there is often unquestioned and prompt access. While these forms of credit often share a number of basic characteristics, there are differences between them, and in order to illustrate this a number are discussed below.

Mail order
Mail order is one of the fastest growing areas of retailing, and within general mail order the growth of credit sales has been substantial. The index of mail order retail sales rose from 100 in 1980 to 160 in 1988. Turnover in 1989 was just under £4 billion.[18] The index of credit sales rose from 100 in 1976 to 308 in 1988. Although mail order is one of the two major forms of credit used by low-income households, most of the retail and credit growth is a result of deliberate attempts by the industry to move 'up market',

and to attract more middle-class customers. In 1987, 31 per cent and 26 per cent of households with yearly incomes of £5,000-£10,000 and £10,000-£15,000 used mail order compared to 21 per cent of those with incomes of under £5,000.[19] In 1990, Berthoud and Kempson confirmed that 'middle income households were the heaviest users of mail-order catalogues', but that amongst low-income borrowers mail order was one of the two most frequently used forms of credit.[20]

In many low-income households, mail order provides the means to purchase clothes, shoes, household goods, toys and presents. Access is 'delivered' directly as individuals are sent catalogues or are shown them by friends or callers (it is also possible to write for a catalogue from a newspaper advertisement). Credit is granted by filling out an order form. Credit referencing has traditionally been minimal or absent and to a large extent this remains the case (see Table 8). The credit is marketed in terms of the cost per week, enabling customers to calculate whether or not they can afford the particular figure, and the credit is notionally interest free. Payments are usually made weekly. Further, goods can be returned without question. Against these advantages, the cost of the goods may be higher than those in the shops, the range more limited and the quality variable. Clearly, though, mail order fits well with the resources and budgeting concerns of those on low income where access and affordability accommodate overall cost and reduced quality. Mail order is also the only form of commercial credit open to sixteen- and seventeen-year-olds, and a third of this age group use it.[21] Its importance to the poorest young adults, unemployed with a very low level of benefit or none at all, is clear.[22]

Check trading and money-lending
Check trading involves national and provincial credit companies (for example, Provident or Shop-a-Check) selling checks with a cash value (typically up to £100) that can be exchanged for goods. Purchases are sometimes restricted to specific shops, but the lender profits from both the loan and commission from the sale of the goods. Repayments are typically made over six months, usually collected weekly by the trader who may, at the same time, also sell additional checks. Credit screening, where it takes place,

is an informal process (undertaken by the collector who judges the sum to lend), but as a consequence the cost of checks can range from 60-200 APR.

However, low-income households may periodically require money rather than goods and turn to finance houses and particularly to money-lenders. As noted earlier, these may be legally registered or illegal loan sharks. There are currently some 5,000 registered money-lenders with an annual turnover in excess of £600 million. They offer small unsecured loans, easy access, negotiation within your own home, rapid decisions and low repayments, collected weekly, usually over a 12-month period. The costs, however, are substantial, as can be seen from Table 10. These results come from a survey of nine registered money-lenders conducted by Birmingham consumer protection officers and the Birmingham Settlement Money Advice Centre.

Borrowers were repaying between £4 and £60 per week and the average charge was 525 APR. Even excluding the uncharacter-istically high costs of lenders 6 and 8, average APR was 257. The annual percentage rate (APR) is the measure used in Britain to indicate the cost of credit. Theoretically it allows borrowers to make comparisons between credit offers while encouraging creditors to act competitively, producing a downward pressure on interest rates, so precluding excessive costs. In practice, few people understand or use APR, preferring to consider the sum payable each week/month.[23] In addition, CCA(UK) argue that APR comparisons systematically flatter the banks and finance houses because, for example, the APR quoted for money-lenders includes the creditors' collection costs. Banks and the like do not have such costs in their APR calculation because they are the responsibility of the borrower. Nevertheless, they *are* costs, and thus it could be argued that APR does not always tell the whole story; that in reality the gulf between APR on bank credit and money-lenders' loans is reduced. While this argument has some substance, its impact is to narrow rather than abolish the gap between the costs of the different forms of credit, and money-lenders remain amongst the most expensive creditors.

Low-income households may also borrow from illegal lenders. This issue was touched on earlier in this chapter and is discussed again in Chapter 5.

TABLE 10
Characteristics of loans offered by money-lenders in the West Midlands (December 1987)

Money-lender	Loan term in weeks	Advance £	Total repayable £	APR %
Money-lender 1	28	50	70.00	258.66
Money-lender 2	25	50	68.97	288.26
	50	100	149.90	142.57
Money-lender 3	20	50	64.00	256.69
	50	100	150.00	143.13
Money-lender 4	20	£10 up to £1,000	–	288.00
	28	£10 up to £1,000	–	240.00
	52	£10 up to £1,000	–	154.00
Money-lender 5	48	Various	–	143-186
	60	Various	–	128-148
Money-lender 6	26	100	142.00	Quoted as 54 Actually 835.5 (when brokerage fee included)
Money-lender 7	18	98	126.00	318.00
	28	98	140.00	
Money-lender 8	14	40	75.00	4822.00
Money-lender 9	29	50	29 at 2.50	294.00

SOURCE: Birmingham Settlement Money Advice Centre

Low-income households which seek commercial credit to meet basic needs are channelled into a high-cost credit market by exclusionary practices that are most complete in the case of bank credit, but which reduce as costs rise through finance company loans to check trading and money-lenders. The last two forms of credit are, with the exception of cost, structured in ways which might be argued to be 'adapted' to the circumstances and budgeting practices of poor households. The limited resources available to such households may make credit use a necessity. However, the costs 'can result in a worsening, rather than an improvement of their financial affairs. Indeed, this group are very vulnerable to being exploited by credit suppliers'.[24]

Outside the commercial sector, alternative forms of credit are available – for example, credit unions and the social fund loan system. The latter interest-free form of credit is specifically targeted at some of the poorest groups in our society and is potentially very important. It is therefore considered briefly below, but only in terms of its operation as a credit system. (There is now considerable research available on the social fund in its entirety. This literature is drawn upon but not reviewed.[25])

The social fund loan system

Since April 1988, credit has been available primarily to those living in poverty in the form of the social fund loan system. Crisis loans and budgeting loans are available (forming 70 per cent of the discretionary budget, with the remaining 30 per cent allocated to community care grants). These payments and loans replaced the previous system of single payments. Claimants become eligible for consideration for a budgeting loan once they have completed twenty-six weeks on income support. Loans are repaid by deductions from benefit 'at source'. Crisis loans are available to both claimants *and* non-claimants – for example, those in work but in or near poverty.

The introduction of the social fund, and particularly the loans, reflected the growing emphasis of successive Conservative governments on altering what, by 1987, they described as the 'benefit culture'. This culture, they argue, could be clearly seen in the increase in single payments' claims in the mid-1980s. Via the social fund, resources would be better targeted on those 'really' in need and welfare dependency would be reduced in favour of individual provision and responsibility. As a form of financing, credit dovetails well with these requirements, since it is individually contracted and involves individuals accepting responsibility for meeting repayments. In the case of the poor, it is a means of converting a structural disadvantage into a personal responsibility.

Putting aside the ideology, how does the social fund stand up as a credit system? Does it meet the needs of the poor and how does it relate to the low-income commercial credit system? Debating this issue in 1989, prior to the availability of much empirical data on the workings of the social fund system, Berthoud set out some of the possibilities.

> In the United Kingdom, it has ... been shown that people on benefit already use credit to a considerable extent. But it is not clear what the importance of that is for the proposal to offer more loans. It could be argued that claimants find credit a useful budgeting tool, and that a new source charging no interest can do them no harm, and might be helpful. The decision to deduct a fixed proportion of benefit to repay loans regardless of their size suggests that the social fund may be more attractive than the commercial market if the loan is a big one, but less attractive the smaller the size of the advance.
> ...But an alternative response to the evidence that claimants already use credit might be that the offer of further advances might add to a claimant's indebtedness. If it did, the problems could be serious: the social fund will place itself first in the queue for repayments, and the debtor's room for manoeuvre in negotiations with other creditors would therefore be restricted.[26]

Nearly two years on, more empirical data are available and some answers are beginning to emerge. Data from a number of projects suggest that the potential disadvantages outlined by Berthoud and others have materialised. In practice, the loan system embodies many of the least desirable characteristics of a credit system as far as low-income households are concerned:

– exclusions operate;[27]
– amongst the eligible, access is delayed;[28]
– collection is inflexible;[29]
– weekly income and budgeting flexibility are reduced;[30]
– applicants feel demeaned.[31]

In addition, because of the way social fund loans curtail income and budgeting flexibility, and worsen the household's financial position, the system clearly creates a pressure for poor households to continue within or re-enter the commercial sector. A number of snapshots drawn from research on the social fund are presented below. They offer a taste of the kinds of situations faced by claimants and illustrate the processes identified above.

Reducing weekly income. 'Mr C is a single pensioner who lives alone. In spite of his disability and age (both high priority criteria) Mr C's application for a community care grant for a fridge, clothing and shoes was refused and he was offered a budgeting loan of £150. Mr C's weekly income support is £51.21. His loan repayments will reduce that amount by £7.68 per week for the next 20 weeks.'[32]

Delayed access. 'Mr I is unemployed with five children. He requests help (from Social Services) to buy food. The need has arisen because Mrs I had to go into hospital and needed items of clothing. An application to the social fund was made but classified as medium priority. The decision ... therefore had to wait until the end of the month and would depend on the state of the budget...'[33]

Entry to the commercial sector. A woman who requested a loan but was excluded on the grounds that the budget was spent said: 'I am angry that having been refused help from the social I must seek a loan from the Provident who charge very high interest.'[34]

Reduced flexibility. 'Mrs A is a single parent. She has two children and multiple debts. The family is short of clothing and bedding. She has applied to the social fund and been awarded a loan. It is unclear how she will now keep up her payments to other debtors which include a money lender.'[35]

Increasing poverty. Ms D 'is a single parent with two children ... was given a budgeting loan of £75 at weekly repayments of £9.71. Her weekly IS is £64.75. Since taking the loan, Ms D reported regularly going without food herself in order to feed the children and meet the bills. The loss of almost £10 a week from the family's meagre income was causing other debts to pile up; the milk bill, increasing use of food "on tick" from local shops, unpaid electricity bill'.[36]

Exclusion 'Mrs E is a single parent in need of clothing and bedding. She has been refused a loan as she is not credit worthy'.[37] '...a number of people who have been completely without money, have had no help available from other resources and were clearly at risk ... were refused crisis loans because they had no money with which to repay.'[38]

From the available evidence, it must be doubted whether the social fund loan system has many benefits for low-income families. Assuming for a moment that a household has some ability to repay a loan, other than cost this system has few of the characteristics required by low-income households, and such characteristics frequently outweigh cost considerations. However, given the current level of income support, it is also clear that many households do not have adequate resources to repay any loan, yet this same lack of resources forces them to borrow. The incorporation within the welfare 'safety net' of a system of loans that results in people living below the safety-net level has been widely challenged. In essence, researchers have argued 'the absurdity of assessing the credit worthiness of those in need'.[39]

NOTES
1. This issue is discussed further in J Ford, *The Indebted Society*, Routledge, 1988.
2. R Berthoud and E Kempson, *Credit and Debt in Britain: First Findings*, Policy Studies Institute, 1990.
3. National Consumer Council, *Consumers and Credit*, NCC, 1980.
4. M Adler and E Wozniak, *The Origins and Consequences of Default*, Research Report for the Scottish Law Commission, 1981.
5. P Ashley, *The Money Problems of the Poor*, Heinemann, 1983.
6. Public Attitude Surveys, *The Consumer's Use of Credit*, 1987.
7. National Consumer Council, *Credit and Debt, The Consumer Interest*, 1990.
8. S Becker, 'Women's Poverty and Social Services', in H Graham and J Popay (eds), *Women and Poverty*, Warwick University and Thomas Coram Institute, 1989.
9. J Bradshaw and H Holmes, *Living on the Edge: A Study of the Living Standards of Families on Benefit in Tyne and Wear*, Tyneside CPAG, 1989.
10. See, for example, E Evason *et al*, *The Deserving and Undeserving Poor*, CPAG (Northern Ireland), 1989; or S McKenna and J Gurney, *In Hock to the State*, Leicester CPAG, 1988.
11. S Bolchever, S Stewart and G Clyde, 'Consumer Credit: Investigating the Loan Sharks', *Trading Standards Review*, Vol 98, No 1.
12. *See* note 11.
13. G Parker, 'Making Ends Meet: Women, Credit and Debt', in C Glendinning and J Millar (eds), *Women and Poverty in Britain*, Wheatsheaf, 1987.
14. M Tebbutt, *Making Ends Meet: Pawnbroking and Working Class Credit*, Leicester University Press, 1983.

15. J Toporowski, 'Beyond Banking: Financial Institutions and the Poor', in P Golding (ed), *Excluding the Poor*, CPAG Ltd, 1987.
16. *Social Trends 1991*, HMSO, 1991.
17. *See* notes 3 and 6.
18. *Business Monitor*, 1989.
19. *See* note 6.
20. *See* note 2.
21. *See* note 6.
22. S McCrae, *Young and Jobless*, Policy Studies Institute, 1987.
23. *See* note 6.
24. *See* note 6.
25. G Craig and J Coxall, *Monitoring the Social Fund: a Bibliography 1985-1989*, University of Bradford, Applied Social Studies Department, 1989.
26. R Berthoud, *Poverty, Credit and Debt*, HMSO, 1989.
27. S Ward, 'Efficient and Effective?', in G Craig (ed), *Your Flexible Friend?*, Social Security Consortium, 1989.
28. *See* note 10.
29. *See* note 10.
30. *See* note 10.
31. C Davies, 'Issues for the Claimant', in G Craig (ed), *Your Flexible Friend?*, Social Security Consortium, 1989.
32. S McKenna and J Gurney, *see* note 10.
33. E Evason *et al*, *see* note 10.
34. *See* note 33.
35. *See* note 33.
36. *See* note 32.
37. *See* note 33.
38. *See* note 27.
39. *See* note 33.

3. LOW INCOME AND DEBT

There is now considerable evidence that the level of debt is increasing in the United Kingdom as a whole.[1] However, the *extent* to which the overall level has risen in the 1980s is a subject of some debate. Equally, it is not clear whether the risk of default has risen to the same degree (or at all) on all forms of credit and expenses, although the rise in some areas (for example, mortgage loans) is certainly a percentage rise. A distinct, but related, issue concerns the distribution of any increase in debt across the different socio-economic groups and household structures.

Such questions arise for many reasons. For example, there are no appropriate time series data available for the 1970s and 1980s on which to base comparisons, so conclusions have to be drawn by piecing together a variety of studies that are not always directly comparable. Different studies often adopt different definitions of debt. Court statistics – often cited to indicate a change in the extent of debt – may reflect changing creditor practices with regard to judicial recovery, while statistics from the advice agencies (showing an increase in the number of debt cases handled) may in part be a reflection of a growing awareness of their services.

All these difficulties need to be kept in mind when considering the statistics presented below. However, on balance, the evidence favours the view that there has been an increase in the incidence of households in debt, but not necessarily with regard to every type of creditor or every type of credit commitment. This chapter briefly presents the general trends with regard to debt and considers how debt is distributed throughout society. The evidence indicates that debt is closely associated with poverty, and that the growth in debt is closely (but not solely) connected with the growth in poverty, particularly in households with children. Those with low incomes have to borrow to secure basic needs, but in many instances their incomes are too low to sustain repayments. In addition to consumer credit default, debt can occur from the failure to pay for services – for example, housing, fuel, water rates, and poll tax. Poverty results in debt, but debt also triggers other processes and responses – financial, personal, social and legal. These processes often increase the vulnerability of those already disadvantaged and further marginalises them. Some of the ways in which this comes about will be considered towards the end of the chapter.

The growth of debt

Berthoud has estimated that in 1981 approximately 1.3 million households were in debt, 130,000 owing money to at least three creditors.[2] According to the PSI survey, by 1989 2.4 million households had had problem debts in the previous year, 560,000 (almost 3 per cent of households) owing to three or more creditors. 'For 170,000 households, the situation was very serious indeed, with five or more debts.'[3] An earlier study, concerned only with Scotland, noted 'that for an increasing number of people there is indeed a problem (and potentially a very serious one)'.[4]

With regard to specific areas of debt, housing debt is substantial. For example, in 1984 the Audit Commission reported that 8 per cent of local authority tenants in England and Wales (roughly 350,000 households) had arrears of three or more months.[5] Figures for Scotland in the mid-1980s indicated that the position was 'appreciably worse'.[6] In 1990, Berthoud and Kempson indicated that 16 per cent of tenants had 'problems' with rent arrears in Britain, and that the situation was worse in Northern Ireland ('problem' debts are debts that respondents were worried about and had difficulty paying). Clearly, these sets of figures are not directly comparable, but they are certainly suggestive of a growth in debt.

The percentage of mortgage loans in arrears of two and more months has also risen from 4.95 per cent (295,000 loans) in 1985 to above 6 per cent (in excess of 530,000 loans) in 1990.[7] Gas and electricity debts are also significant. The level of disconnection is one indication of debt. On this basis the number of debtors has fallen. There were 35,166 gas disconnections in 1980. The number rose in the mid-1980s but by 1988/89 had fallen to 19,379.[8]

Typically consumers are disconnected owing around seven months' payments. The drop in disconnections is in large part the result of changes to the methods of payment and the greater use of pre-paid meters which are used both to prevent further debt and recoup arrears. Electricity disconnections have also fallen during the 1980s from 98,894 in 1979/80 to 72,230 in 1988/89.[9] Pre-paid meters and other pre-payment schemes are in use. Of concern in Scotland, and of potential concern in England and Wales, is the level of default on the community charge. In Scotland, in 1989/90 non-payment ran at about a third of the amount due. Comparable figures for mid-1990/91 suggest a non-payment level slightly higher than in the previous year. In May 1990, almost 2,500 income support claimants in Scotland had direct deductions from benefit for arrears on their poll tax payments.[10] The position in England is highly variable, with non-payment ranging from 51 per cent in Liverpool to 3.6 per cent in Plymouth.[11] In many areas, poll tax default exceeds the default level previously seen on the rates, although while all non-payment is debt, clearly some of this is politically motivated rather than reflecting an inability to pay.

County court statistics record an increase in plaints entered by banks and finance houses to recover money loans from 132,000 in 1981 to 160,000 in 1985. Recent data on the changes in default on many other forms of consumer credit agreements are not available. The banks and finance houses provide little data about credit card debts. Nevertheless, in the mid-1980s the Finance Houses Association indicated that, although the numbers in default to their members had grown, the proportion of borrowers in default had not.[12]

Routes into debt

Although there is a small number of people who are in debt because of an unwillingness to pay their bills (for whatever reason) despite having adequate resources to do so, most debt results from a failure of income to match expenditure commitments. However, this situation can arise for a number of different reasons. Some people (although probably only a small proportion of debtors) find credit difficult to resist and become 'voluntarily' overcommitted. This problem is sometimes associated with what Caplovitz has called credit-card mania.[13] More frequently, debt results from either a sudden disruption to income (for example, as a result of unemployment or relationship breakdown or illness), where previous commitments are difficult to sustain, or from a slower, cumulative effect of a persistently low and inadequate income (for example, as a result of living on benefit for a sustained period), and it is these two processes that have been so pronounced during the 1980s.

The processes of slow decline and sudden disruption are conceptually distinct, although in practice linked for many households. For a proportion of those who lose income unexpectedly the situation will be temporary. They will be re-employed or rehoused in a situation which allows them to re-establish the income and expenditure balance and discharge any debts that developed. Others, however, may find it difficult to obtain new work and will be forced to rely on benefit. Others may be re-employed but only within the casual low-paid sector. In these instances, any initial drop in income will continue and living standards will be further eroded. These processes, the connections between them and some of their consequences for further borrowing are clearly shown in the quotation below taken from Gillian Parker's research on unemployment and debt:

> The recently unemployed household starts to take on credit, presumably for items which previously would have been bought with cash, begins to experience difficulty meeting housing costs and starts to miss fuel bills. As unemployment continues beyond the twelve months, the family borrows money (perhaps as a reaction to the increased amounts needed to service credit commitments), and falls into arrears with housing payments (perhaps to allow unpaid fuel bills to be met). By the time unemployment has stretched to over twelve months the only credit granters likely to 'take on' such families are the club and check traders who charge more for their services, thus tightening an already vicious circle.[14]

The distribution of debt

A low-income issue?

During the 1980s and early 1990s, evidence has been accumulating to support the association between low income, specific household structures and debt. In particular, the presence of children and the number of children within the household have come to be recognised as a more central influence than low income *per se*. Research undertaken in Scotland in 1981 highlighted 'the very low incomes indeed' of debtors summonsed in the courts, the association of default with large families as well as the over-representation of lone-parent households compared with their distribution in the population as a whole.[15] Following an analysis of data drawn from council tenants in 1981, Berthoud concluded:

> Comparisons between families at different income levels but with the same family composition suggests that the pure effect of income is less than might be expected ... indebtedness tends to affect families which have both low income and children.[16]

Unemployed, low-income families have been shown to be particularly vulnerable and almost every study shows that a large number of debtors are claimants.[17]

More recent data on the distribution of debt come from two of the surveys discussed earlier – PAS (1987) and Berthoud and Kempson (1990) (the PSI study). At the time of writing, only the preliminary results are available for the latter study, but even so, the general pattern of the distribution of debt can be identified. Some important differences between these two surveys were outlined in the footnotes to Table 7. Both surveys show the continuing importance of the relationship between low income and debt that was noted at the start of the decade. They also suggest an increase in the *extent* of low-income debt.

The surveys indicate that debt is most heavily concentrated in the lower income groups. In 1987, 20 per cent of those with incomes between £50 and £99 per week and 17 per cent with incomes between £100 and £199 per week had experienced problems paying, compared to 10 per cent of those with incomes of £400+ per week. Table 11 shows the findings from the PSI survey. In 1990, 27.8 per cent of households with net weekly income of under £100 had debts, compared to 8.4 per cent of households in the £300-£400 weekly income bracket.

TABLE 11
Incidence of debt, by income group (all non-pensioner households)

Net weekly income	Percentage with debts	Mean no. of debts
Up to £100	27.8	0.56
£100 to £150	24.8	0.51
£150 to £200	14.8	0.27
£200 to £250	10.5	0.22
£250 to £300	11.1	0.22
£300 to £400	8.4	0.15
£400 or more	3.1	0.05
Average	14.6	0.29

SOURCE: PSI (1990) Credit and Debt in Britain: First Findings

Thus, both surveys show that debt affects a greater percentage of low-income households than better-off households and reverses the pattern identified in Chapter 1 (Table 6) with respect to credit use. Compared to high-income households, fewer low-income households use credit and those which use credit use less. However, it is amongst low-income households that debt problems are concentrated. This finding highlights not only the vulnerability to problems amongst the poorer households, but also confirms that debt can emerge in the absence of credit, as when housing and other service bills are not paid. Further support for the association between low income and debt comes from a 1987 study which examined the clients of money advice centres. Eighty-three per cent had incomes under £150 a week. Even though the clients of money advice centres may not be representative of debtors as a whole, the coincidence of poverty and debt is hard to escape.[18]

The PSI survey also draws attention to the impact of the number of credit commitments on debt. (For PSI, a credit commitment is a bank loan, store or credit card, etc. Mortgages are treated as household expenses.) This relationship varies by income, but specifically amongst low-income households the greater the number of credit commitments, the greater the debts:

> Poorer households with no credit commitments did not have many debts; but the more their commitments the more their debts. In the small group with low income and three or more consumer credit commitments, 39 per cent of the sample reported debts, with an average of 2.5 problems each.[19]

Considering the pressures on low-income budgets, it is not surprising that debt can exist in the absence of credit nor that if there are additional credit commitments the financial pressures are even greater and debt even more likely.

Both the PAS and PSI surveys stress the prevalence of debt amongst households with children under 16. For example, less than a third of households interviewed by PAS had children under 16, but amongst those reporting difficulties with payments, more than half were households with children. Berthoud and Kempson (1990) note the exceptional level of risk amongst lone parents.

The unemployed also experience more debts than many other groups. However, debts appear to be greater for those households where the head of the household had worked at some time during the previous three years but was unemployed at the time of the survey.

> The level of serious debt ... was even higher for this group than for those who had been unemployed for the whole of the previous three years.[20]

Those who have intermittent, casual employment may face downward pressure on their wages, and have no entitlement to redundancy pay, holiday or sick pay. Unlike those who experience unemployment but have some redundancy money to put towards their commitments, casual workers may face periods of unemployment with little or no financial cushion. When they work, their wages may be little different from benefit levels, yet income from employment rather than benefit may alter the help available to them. A clear example is the case of low-income owner-occupiers in arrears with their mortgage payments. Most of those in work cannot receive help with mortgage interest payments. This help is available to mortgagors on supplementary benefit/income support and 207,000 were claiming in 1986. Low-income home owners in low-waged, casual work are one of the groups particularly vulnerable to debt.[21]

Types of debt

The most problematic areas of debt can also be identified from the two surveys. The PAS data identify the percentage of users of different types of credit reporting difficulties. The highest incidence of difficulties is with loans from finance companies (16 per cent of users reported difficulties) and check trading agreements (14 per cent). These are both forms of credit typically taken by low-income households, the latter almost exclusively, although increasingly 'loans from finance houses may be more likely to be obtained by people who possibly could not get other forms of credit simply because they are regarded as not being a good credit risk'.[22] PSI adopt a similar procedure, expressing the incidence of debt as a proportion of those with each type of commitment. This is called the 'risk of debt'. However, the wider remit of the PSI study results in some difference in the findings (see Table 7). The risk of debt is highest with regard to rent payments – 16 per cent of tenants have problematic rent debts and, as can be seen from Figure 3, this level of risk is at least twice that incurred for any other commitment. The next most problematic areas are overdrafts (8 per cent), and loans where over 5 per cent of users had debts. Included in this last category are loans from finance houses, money-lenders or tallymen, check companies and pawnbrokers, as well as bank and building society loans. Some of these forms of credit are used exclusively or predominantly by low-income borrowers. However, understanding the exact distribution of debts on loans from these diverse sources by income group will only be possible when the full results of the PSI study are available.

The surveys build a consistent picture concerning debt and indicate a clear association between debt and low income, particularly where there are children. Amongst the poor, it is

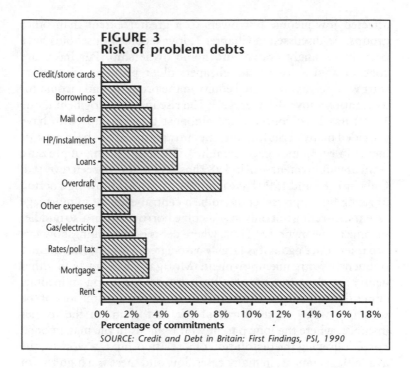

FIGURE 3
Risk of problem debts

Credit/store cards
Borrowings
Mail order
HP/instalments
Loans
Overdraft
Other expenses
Gas/electricity
Rates/poll tax
Mortgage
Rent

0%   2%   4%   6%   8%   10% 12% 14% 16% 18%
Percentage of commitments
SOURCE: Credit and Debt in Britain: First Findings, PSI, 1990

principally lone parents or households with children where the head of household is unemployed or intermittently employed who find themselves in debt. The high proportion of these groups that are tenants (particularly in the local authority sector) results in rent arrears being particularly common; debts to finance houses, money-lenders and check traders are also important, but less frequent.

Home-owners and mortgage arrears

Although several sources indicate the substantial extent of debt amongst tenants, it is important to draw attention to owner-occupiers who, in general, are better off, more likely to use credit and less likely to have housing and other debts. However, as already noted, mortgage default rose during the 1980s and it affected low-income borrowers to a greater extent than other groups. As discussed in Chapter 1, low-income households have been increasingly drawn into home ownership. Purchases are concentrated amongst the cheaper, older property; borrowers start with relatively limited equity in the property and income-to-loan ratios above the average.[23] The rise in unemployment in the 1980s has been concentrated amongst those groups who have provided many of the low-income entrants and it has been a major factor in rising mortgage default.[24] The slight easing of pressure from unemployment seen in 1989 has, by late 1990, been reversed. Only in 1989 and 1990 have interest-rate rises (following a period of rising house prices) come to be a central element in mortgage arrears, affecting not only low-income borrowers but also middle-income home owners.[25] Thus, where debts occur amongst owner-occupiers once again it is largely associated with low income and frequently with unemployment. Mortgage arrears (and other debts) are also often the result of a household losing an income, either through relationship breakdown or through the loss of the woman's wage on the birth of the first child. In the former instance, where the lone parent who remains in the matrimonial home following the dissolution of a relationship is a woman, the available income is, in many cases, low and there is a high risk of mortgage default.[26] Those who are reliant on income support are eligible for help with mortgage interest payments. However, there is some evidence that quite often this money has to be 'diverted' to meet more pressing needs, thus increasing the risk of losing the property.[27]

While in many instances debt is associated with poverty, not all those in poverty face an identical situation, or respond to their situation in similar ways. Income and expenditure may be differently structured and situated in different social and cultural contexts. The absence of pensioners from the discussion of credit and debt is one useful reminder of this situation. For example, pensioner households have different demands because of the absence of young children; they may have different and fewer needs than young couples, but they also adopt rather different attitudes to credit and debt that curtail involvement.[28] In addition, during the 1980s the benefits available to many pensioners were more generous than those to other groups. Developing a more complete understanding of the specific form of the processes that influence credit use and engender debt amongst different sectors of the poor is an important but as yet incomplete task.

The remainder of this chapter considers some aspects of the response of households to their debt; first the pressures to take further credit to borrow their way out of debt, and then the personal and social consequences of debt.

The financial implications of debt – more credit

There is considerable evidence that those with debts often attempt to solve their problems by taking further credit. Many people borrow from friends and relatives, but here the discussion is about the use of formal credit to manage debt. Developments in the credit market have been such as both to encourage and respond to this possibility. Credit for those in debt can be obtained in both the commercial and extortionate markets – commercially through registered money-lenders and the finance houses, and in some cases the banks and building societies; at usurious rates from unregistered loan sharks. Loans may either be 'secured' or 'unsecured'. Two possible forms of lending are discussed below – secured loans in the commercial market and then unsecured loans as provided by both money-lenders and loan sharks.

Secured lending

Commercial credit is divided into secured and unsecured lending. The former includes mortgages, but also money loans secured on land (houses) for purposes other than house purchase. Such loans are sometimes referred to as 'a second charge on the property'. Secured loans can be applied for by anyone with an existing house and the majority are used by solvent borrowers to undertake home improvements. They are mainly offered by the finance houses, the banks and building societies. Secured lending, however, is also offered to those with existing debts.

In 1987, the National Consumer Council commissioned research on secured lending and their results provide an important source of data on this sector.[29] The research involved a national survey of home owners and a consideration of cases of secured lending drawn from money advice agencies. The survey indicated that there were around a million secured loans in operation, the majority (79 per cent) taken from the banks and building societies. Only 16 per cent came from the finance houses (although the NCC suggest there are good reasons to believe that this is an underestimate). The majority of loans were used in connection with home improvements. Only 50,000 (5 per cent) of these loans were originally taken to pay off existing debts.

Where debtors are explicitly targeted and offered 'consolidation' loans, the form of the offer can appear attractive on a number of counts:

– the lack of restrictions on the use of the money;
– debt as an explicit criterion for access;
– decisions are instant;
– few, if any, enquiries are made about income;
– one payment replaces several which suggests that overall this will be a cheaper form of borrowing.

And finally, of course, temporarily borrowers are no longer 'in debt'. Instead, they are 'credit users' and this change, at least for the moment, may remove a stigma. Secured loans offer an apparent solution.

However, evidence to suggest some problems with secured loans is provided by the 114 cases from money advice centres that were considered in the NCC survey. These indicate that, in comparison with the profile of secured loans as a whole, it is loans taken out to manage existing debts that become problems. A third of problem loans had been taken specifically to pay off other debts (5 per cent in the national survey). A third of borrowers were in households where net weekly income was £100 or less, and only 25 per cent had incomes over £150 per week. Defaulters tended to be married with dependants. Whereas a minority of all secured loans was provided by the finance houses, according to the survey 75 per cent of the problem loans were from finance houses. Thus the picture builds up to one of low-income borrowers with debts taking secured loans, mainly from finance houses, and experiencing considerable default. The secured loan may have replaced all previous debts, or borrowers may also have other creditors, notably a mortgage lender to whom they may also owe money. The study also draws attention to the finding that amongst the money advice clients even those whose secured loan was not specifically taken to pay off other debts, financial difficulties were already evident.

Two further issues are important in considering the use of secured loans by the poor and particularly by those already in debt. One is cost and the other is the growth of financial intermediaries. Data on the APR charged was documented from advertisements. The range was 11.4 to 23.1 per cent, but there appeared to be many extra costs (insurance, brokerage fees, etc). The report says, 'Clearly people in debt would be charged substantially higher APR.' This tendency can be seen from the problem loans. Here the range was 13 to 44 per cent.[30]

The average loan was nearly £4,500 when first taken out, but the range was from £400-£20,000. At this stage, a majority of borrowers, many of whom had been in financial difficulties prior to taking out these loans, were repaying an average of £75 a month, on incomes frequently under £100 a week. Just under 50 per cent of the loans had been arranged through brokers. While this figure cannot be compared to any from the national survey, the important fact to note is the additional costs of access as a result of this process. Examples from the NCC study are £800 on a £2,000 loan; £1,500 on a £6,500 loan; £600 on a £20,000 loan (see also the case study on page 64).

Thus, those who decide to borrow because they have debts can obtain access to further credit, but only at a cost that must always cast doubt on their ability to repay. Such repayment as takes place must be significantly detrimental to their living standards. Data from both the NCC study and other studies indicate that secured lending of this type can quickly result in legal proceedings and the loss of the property on which the loan is secured. There has been considerable discussion of the extent to which the term 'secured' loan may mislead people into thinking the loan is 'secure', particularly given the relatively low levels of financial knowledge found in all social groups.[31] One recent development has been the introduction of a 'health warning' when such loans are advertised and granted, but as yet there is little indication of their effectiveness. Just under half of the cases considered from advice agencies as part of the NCC study were at the actual or threatened stage of legal proceedings, with creditors attempting to possess these homes. The following case study (derived from a report in the *Independent*) illustrates some of the processes discussed above, and the growing vulnerability of those who, through poverty, use credit and fall into debt.

Case study: Secured lending to repay debts

Following redundancy, Reg Hill had substantial mortgage arrears on his local authority mortgage loan. Replying to an advertisement, he inquired about an urgent loan and remortgage and was visited by a credit broker. 'We wanted to clear our debts and have about £3,000 left to do repairs.' Reg Hill was told that because the arrears cast doubt on his credit worthiness he would have to have a 'bridging mortgage' for a few months and then be placed with a building society in the normal way. Reg Hill signed up for a four-month bridge produced by a finance company. The costs were:

Redemption of existing mortgage	£12,768.37
Repay bank	£1,200.00
Fee to credit broker	£4,259.63
Four-month interest in advance	£3,472.00
Total	£21,700.00

After four months a building society mortgaged Reg Hill, lending £24,500 (£21,700 to pay off the bridge and £3,000 for improvements). In the event, only £19,000 could be repaid to the finance company (the mortgage was an endowment mortgage with 'up front' premiums, and involved an arrangement fee, all met out of the £24,500). Commitments had increased from £12,768 plus £2,118 arrears to £24,500 plus a £2,500 debt. Income in the meantime had remained constant. Reg Hill quickly found he could not meet the building society payments, and possession proceedings were taken.

Unsecured credit

Debtors without property against which further credit can be secured have little choice but to take unsecured loans at high costs, either in the commercial market or the extortionate market. In the case of the former, data already presented in Table 10 showed that the loans made by licensed money-lenders in Birmingham to the unemployed and welfare recipients carried an average APR of 525 per cent and consolidation loans (ie, one loan replacing several including arrears) are likely to be among the most expensive. Unsecured lending is a substantial activity. In reporting this study, Conaty notes that in 1987 one of the largest companies in the survey had an annual turnover of £37 million in the Birmingham region alone.[32] However, the costs of such loans are likely to lead to repayment problems, particularly for families with low incomes. In the extortionate market, loan sharks make even higher charges and the use of some illegal recovery practices are reported, usually by trading standards or consumer protection departments of the local authorities. One such report said:

> The department has received reports of 'heavies' being used to ensure repayment of debt, and there is evidence of people so involved in debt that there is no foreseeable release from it beyond receiving something like a win on the football pools... Reports have been received of 'factory gate' collectors who station themselves handily on pay day to ensure repayment of debt.[33]

Social and personal implications of debt

At a personal level, debt reinforces and intensifies the experience of poverty but adds a further dimension that stems from the fact of debt itself. These experiences have implications not only for people's material well-being but also for their self-esteem and their relationships with other household members as well as wider social contacts. Individuals and households who are in debt experience constant anxiety about money and have to economise further on an already inadequate budget. They also frequently feel ashamed by the situation they find themselves in:

'I felt ashamed about getting into trouble with the rent...'[34]

'I feel guilty about what has happened – I feel so embarrassed, it's a mark on me.'[35]

One person, interviewed by John Brady in his study of families in debt, summed up the sense of many other qualitative accounts by saying that it was like 'being in a tunnel with no light to get out'.[36]

This sense of helplessness, sometimes along with resignation, pervades many accounts of the experience of debt. Again Brady's respondents told him 'I can't see any end. I can't see any hope,' and 'after the first year I thought it might get better but it just gets worse'.

This personal response to debt has its roots not only in the material deprivation experienced, but also in societal attitudes that still view debt as a personal failure, a stigma or a sign of incompetence, even while recognising to a greater extent than previously the impact of structural factors such as unemployment.[37] Debtors consistently report that they feel ashamed of their situation, that they 'know' they will be judged as failures or incompetent, to the point where they may attempt to hide it from others or feel inhibited about seeking help either from creditors or advice agencies. In a study of unemployed families, McKee provides an account of how some of those with debts felt they were viewed or treated by their families:

> Last week we had to sell the stereo and we decided to go and see Mum. We just didn't want to go through it. It's a whole scene. She starts moaning: 'You should do this and you should do that' and 'if you hadn't given your job up'... You know, you just go through the whole scene. You just feel like the lowest of the low anyway.[38]

Another study reported a family in which both partners had been made redundant, but would not ask for help because they feared they would be made to feel the situation was a result of their own mismanagement, an assessment that the quote shows they were in danger of accepting:

> They'd only say you shouldn't have done this, you shouldn't have done that. I've tried and I've failed – that's it.[39]

As a result, there are many cases where the burden of debt is borne at least initially within the confines of the household, with significant consequences for household relations. Debtors often point to a deterioration in their relationships with both partners and children. These become stressful and antagonistic as conflicts and anxieties emerge over how to allocate resources, who should give up what, who is to blame, and what will happen to them.

> 'You say the most hateful things to one another and you know you should not be saying it.' [40]

> 'We argue a lot more now... Sometimes quite heated ... little things now ... about overspending a couple of bob... I mean things that she shouldn't have spent ... at times I've been very strained ... purely lack of money...' [41]

And about the children:

> 'You shout at them all the time, you tend to pick on them.' [42]

Debt may also curtail wider social relationships. A study of families with mortgage arrears indicated that three-quarters of them stopped going out because they could not contribute to the reciprocal nature of much social life. A drink in the pub is both a social and an economic exchange and both may be problematic for those with debts. One respondent commented, 'Social life – forget it. You just can't handle it.' [43]

Another indicated how a fairly restricted social life was further curtailed:

> 'I gave up going to football. I used to travel with the team. We didn't give up much else because we didn't really go out before.' [44]

As a result of these changes, debtors already on the economic margins of our society come to occupy the social margins, a pattern confirmed by a number of studies. [45]

Although some households with debts may be reluctant to ask for help from their kin, it is clear that many do. Borrowing money from parents and other kin on an informal basis is widespread and one of two principal forms of credit used by low-income households.[46] There is also evidence of support in kind. However, support may not be automatic or straightforward, but rather structured by a range of social and cultural factors. McKee [47] indicates that support for unemployed families could depend, for example, on the parents' approval of the marriage partner, or beliefs by both sets of kin about who should provide. Debtors may see help as a necessity, but in conflict with a belief that they should be independent.

> I am an independent person and I like to provide for my own child, but I can't. I will always feel a debt to other people.[48]

> I feel like the poor relation having to rely on my family to buy my son a present.[49]

These conflicts are sometimes resolved or found more acceptable where support is offered in kind.

> ...She'd come over and say 'I've just seen this tin of salmon. Cheaper than anywhere else so I bought it you.' I knew full well it wasn't cheaper, but it didn't seem so bad. Not as bad as accepting money.[50]

Equally, asking for help may be managed in ways which retain as much dignity and privacy as possible. One couple who borrowed from parents when debts mounted commented that 'they'd only know the washer had gone wrong, or the car needed something, not that it was for the gas or the mortgage.' [51]

In some respects, the experience of debt magnifies and reinforces the experience of poverty – the watchfulness and anxiety over money; the calculation and moving around of limited funds. But debt may also alter the agenda. For example, social exclusion may increase; households become vulnerable to legal sanctions and to the loss of any property they possess; homelessness cannot be discounted.

NOTES

1. See, for example, the review of debt in the National Consumer Council, *Credit and Debt: the Consumer Interest*, HMSO, 1990; and M Adler and R Sainsbury, *Personal Debt in Scotland*, Scottish Consumer Council, 1988.
2. R Berthoud, *Poverty, Credit and Debt*, HMSO, 1989.
3. R Berthoud and E Kempson, *Credit and Debt in Britain: First Findings*, Policy Studies Institute, 1990.
4. M Adler and R Sainsbury, *see* note 1.
5. Audit Commission, *Bringing Rent Arrears under Control*, HMSO, 1984.
6. *See* note 4.
7. J Ford, 'National Debts', *Roof*, Vol 15, No 5, 1990.
8. National Consumer Council, *see* note 1.
9. *See* note 8.
10. *House of Commons Hansard*, 2 July 1990, col 460.
11. *The Guardian* newspaper has been regularly monitoring poll tax payments and is the source of the data used here.
12. Finance House Association, *Annual Reports* 1985-1990.
13. D Caplovitz, 'Credit Card Mania', Paper presented to a conference on Unemployment and Debt, Hamburg, 1989.
14. G Parker, 'Unemployment, Low Income and Debt', in I Ramsay (ed), *Debtors and Creditors*, Professional Books, 1986.
15. M Adler and E Wozniak, 'The Origins and Consequences of Default', Research Report for the Scottish Law Commission, No 5, HMSO, 1981.
16. *See* note 2.
17. *See* note 2.
18. A Hartropp *et al*, *Families in Debt*, Jubilee Centre, 1988.
19. *See* note 3.
20. *See* note 3.
21. J Ford, 'Casual Work and Owner Occupation', *Work, Employment and Society*, Vol 3, No 1, 1989.
22. Public Attitude Surveys, *The Consumer's Use of Credit*, 1987.
23. See, for example, V Karn, J Kemeny and P Williams, *Low Income Owner Occupation: Salvation or Despair*, Gower, 1985.
24. J Doling, V Karn and B Stafford, 'The impact of unemployment on home ownership', *Housing Studies*, Vol 1, No 1, 1986.
25. Skipton Building Society, *Report on a survey of mortgage arrears*, 1990.
26. O Sullivan, 'Housing movements of the divorced and separated', *Housing Studies*, Vol 1, No 1, 1986.
27. J Ford, *The Indebted Society*, Routledge, 1988.
28. *See* note 22.
29. National Consumer Council, *Security Risks*, HMSO, 1987.
30. *See* note 29.
31. *See* note 30.
32. P Conaty, 'Credit, Debt and Financial Control', Paper presented to a conference on Unemployment and Debt, Hamburg, 1989.

33. Reported in B Williams, *Cleaning up the Debt Environment,* Jubilee Centre, 1989.
34. L Burghes, *Living from Hand to Mouth,* CPAG/FSU, 1980.
35. *See* note 27.
36. J Brady, *Living in Debt,* Birmingham Settlement Money Advice Centre, 1987.
37. P Rock, *Making People Pay,* Routledge, 1973; *see* also note 15.
38. L McKee, 'Households during Unemployment: the Resourcefulness of the Unemployed', in J Brannen and G Wilson (eds), *Give and Take in Families,* Unwin, 1987.
39. *See* note 27.
40. *See* note 36.
41. J Ritchie, *Thirty Families: Their Living Standards in Unemployment,* Department of Social Security Research Report No 1, HMSO, 1990.
42. *See* note 36.
43. *See* note 27.
44. *See* note 27.
45. For example, see note 34, note 41, and H Graham, 'Being Poor: Perceptions and Coping Strategies of Lone Mothers', in J Brannen and G Wilson (eds), *Give and Take in Families,* Unwin, 1987.
46. *See* note 3.
47. *See* note 38.
48. C Oppenheim and S McEvaddy, *Christmas on the Breadline,* CPAG Ltd, 1987.
49. *See* note 48.
50. *See* note 27.

4. WOMEN, POVERTY AND DEBT

Amongst those in poverty, not all are likely to experience debt, or develop debts to the same extent. The research reviewed in the previous chapters showed the vulnerability to debt of different types of households; it is unemployed households, low-income families with children, and lone parents who are particularly poor and who develop debts to a greater extent than pensioners and non-pensioner households without children. Research has also begun to stress the gendered nature of poverty and demonstrate the degree to which, and ways in which, women are more likely than men to be poor.[1] The causes of women's poverty lie in the sexual division of labour which disadvantages women economically, socially and politically within the household, the labour market and the social security system. Many structures and processes within society assume that women are economically dependent on men. One consequence is that work within the home (predominantly undertaken by women) is neither valued nor adequately rewarded, and labour market opportunities for women are frequently restricted and poorly paid. Thus many women may be vulnerable to poverty whether they live alone, as a lone parent, or within a family with a partner. As a consequence, they may be particularly vulnerable to debt.

This chapter considers some of the ways in which women's poverty gives rise to debt, and the way debt is experienced and managed by women. Women may be poor because the resources entering the household are inadequate, or because there is an unequal distribution of resources within a household, or both. The first possibility is discussed below in relation to lone parents, the overwhelming majority of whom are women.

Lone mothers, poverty and debt

The extent of poverty

Recent figures show that there are approximately 1.1 million lone parents in Britain, of whom 910,000 are lone mothers.[2] The risk of poverty amongst lone parents is higher than for other non-pensioner groups and amongst lone parents, lone mothers have a higher risk of poverty than lone fathers.[3] In 1987, 1.2 million children living in or on the margins of poverty (defined as 140 per cent of SB or below) were living in lone parent families – ie, 76 per cent of all children in lone parent families.[4]

The 1980s have seen an increase in the percentage of lone mothers dependent on state benefits for their income. In 1979, under 320,000 lone mothers were dependent on supplementary benefit. By 1984, this had risen to 491,000, and in 1989 more than 700,000 lone mothers were dependent on income support.[5] The percentage of lone mothers in employment was relatively steady in the mid-1970s and early 1980s at just under 50 per cent. However, between 1982 and 1984 the percentage of lone mothers in employment dropped to 39 per cent, and the drop in women in full-time jobs was particularly marked.[6] A growing percentage of those who work now do so in part-time jobs that are increasingly low paid and often casual in nature. Many part-time jobs are structured in ways which exclude their holders from eligibility for employment protection measures such as redundancy payments, unemployment benefit or sick pay.

For the increasing number of lone mothers claiming benefit, the changes in the social security system over the 1980s have affected the resources available to them. Up until the mid-1980s, lone parents' benefits rose faster than the rate of inflation, although the small gain in real terms still left their incomes at under a third of gross male manual earnings.[7] Since the implementation (in 1988) of the 1986 Social Security Act, the position of lone parents has, in all likelihood, deteriorated. Berthoud calculated that the full proposals were likely to mean losses for 56 per cent of lone parents[8] and a recent assessment by Oppenheim has shown that for a lone parent with a child under five the loss can be 2 per cent in real terms, or 95p per week.[9] A lone parent who is 18 or over with two children aged eight and six currently receives £66.35 per week (1991/92 rates). Evidence to suggest a worsening financial position for lone mothers comes from those who have been monitoring the impact of the social fund on social work and social services departments.[10] Such departments are currently reporting an increase in the number of new referrals with financial difficulties who have failed to obtain help elsewhere (usually from the Department of Social Security). Amongst new referrals (monitored over six week-long periods), 25 per cent were lone parents. Amongst existing clients, 20 per cent were lone parents. Thirty-three per cent of those given 'emergency' help in the form of a loan of equipment or a section 1/12 payment were lone parents.[11]

Lone mothers on low incomes also have little respite from their situation. Research shows that the chance of their improving their economic position is much lower than amongst low-income two-adult households. Comparisons of the position of lone mothers at two points in time (1979 and 1980) showed that over the year 11 per cent had improved their financial position compared to 35 per cent of two-adult households. Employment was the key to the change, but only in conjunction with another household earner. In other words, unless lone mothers enter a household where someone is already earning, and are themselves able to earn, the chances of escaping poverty are limited.[12]

Meeting needs

The resources available to most lone mothers are such that they experience substantial levels of unmet need. Like other people living in poverty, they cannot find the money for larger one-off items (cookers, beds, washing machines, etc). In addition, lone mothers have, over a period of time, reported problems in meeting daily living expenses, particularly as benefit day approaches.[13] The strategies adopted by lone mothers in response to a shortfall in resources aim to safeguard the needs of their children. Lone parents curtail their own consumption of food, fuel, clothes, etc. They accept help from kin and they also borrow in all the credit arenas open to them.

Many of the issues outlined above – low income, one-off

requirements, routine daily shortages – are illustrated in the brief case studies on pages 76-77. The first example comes from a study by Hilary Graham, and shows the very tight budgets typical of many lone mothers. In this case, £41 out of a weekly income of £56 is accounted for in advance, much of it to repay debts. Although the figures refer to 1984, the sense conveyed by the example remains relevant today. The second example concerns a young woman about to become a lone mother. Although her situation is a less typical one, the case study indicates the poor material circumstances under which lone motherhood can start. Although her income will rise when she becomes a lone parent, so will her expenditure. The Finer Committee (1974) calculated that a single parent needed at least two-thirds of the income of a couple with children to make comparable provision.

With regard to the use of credit as a means of budgeting, the possibilities available to lone mothers are structured not only by the income available to them, but by a wider set of policies and procedures adopted towards them. For example, almost two-thirds of lone mothers are local authority tenants (compared to a quarter of two-parent families),[14] often ghettoised by allocation policies in poor property on the poorest estates.[15] Rent and fuel payments are important commitments, but also major resources in the form of proxy credit that can be used temporarily to meet a demand with a higher priority or faster penalty for non-payment. If income remains low, the likelihood of repayment of the 'borrowed' payment decreases. Thus, while some studies of lone mothers report that priority is given to housing and fuel payments, in practice such households have substantial levels of rent and fuel arrears.[16] These arrears then act as a further pressure on the budget, particularly if they are recouped at source from benefit payments as, for example, in 'fuel direct' agreements. This then leaves less income each week for other needs, reduces budgeting flexibility and potentially increases the need to borrow again.

Lone mothers also borrow informally, commercially, from the state and in the extortionate market. For example, lone parents are the highest percentage category of recipients from the social fund – 45 and 51 per cent respectively in 1988/89 and 1989/90.[17] In the commercial market, their position is a highly disadvantageous one. Their credit rating is lowered by their tenure, their frequent location on estates perceived as 'problem' estates, their reliance on benefit or low income and their low occupational status if they are in employment. These factors effectively exclude lone mothers from bank credit, but also in many cases from store cards and finance house loans and result in their using mail order, check trading, doorstep traders and creditors and in some instances loan sharks. Amongst low-income groups, lone parents have one of the highest levels of multiple credit commitments.

Lone mothers and vulnerability to debt

The current vulnerability of lone mothers to debt, vis-à-vis other low-income groups, has recently been indicated by Berthoud and Kempson in the preliminary account of the PSI survey of credit and debt. They comment that low-income lone mothers have an 'exceptional' level of risk.

> More than four out of ten lone parents had one or more problem debt; almost one in seven were in serious debt, owing money on three or more commitments.[18]

A study in Northern Ireland of claimants approaching social services departments showed the particularly severe indebtedness of single parents where three times as many as any other group of claimants had three or more debts. In addition, their position appeared to be one that was worsening over time.[19]

While many lone mothers are vulnerable to debt as a result of persistent low income, there is also evidence of an inability to meet commitments as a result of a sudden drop in income, often following relationship breakdown. Sullivan indicates that divorced and separated women who do not remarry (many of whom are lone mothers) face considerable housing difficulties. Although such women may initially remain in the matrimonial home, the costs often prove prohibitive and debts result. Subsequently, many of these women experience 'forced' moves out of single-owner occupancy into public renting, possibly in a shared capacity, or into homelessness.[20]

Case studies

'I keep an account and work out how much I can afford... If I have rent arrears or like the cooker which was left to pay off when he went ... I pay those, then I work out how much I have left for food. The bills come first ... then the meters ... and then food and then any extra cash for little bits and pieces. If I do have a few quid left over I give it to a neighbour to look after for when I've got a dearer week.'

Out of her weekly income of £56, she pays:

£6.00	HP debt on her cooker
£10.00	debt on her telephone
£25.00	for the electricity and gas meters. The meters are 'timed up' to pay off arrears
£41.00	Total

Lone mother, 1984

SOURCE: H Graham in J Brannen and G Wilson, *Give and Take in Families*

Cindy is 19 years of age and six months pregnant. She has no family and few friends. She receives £31.15 per week income support. From this she must pay for all her clothes, food, entertainment, travel and bills. She recently applied to the social fund for the maternity payment but was turned down because her application was one week early. She has now been told by her local DSS that because of the time it takes to deal with an application she won't receive the £100 grant until after the baby is born.

The health visitor is very concerned about Cindy's health and the development of the baby. The baby does not appear to be large enough for its age. The accommodation is very cold. Cindy is always hungry. The health visitor helped Cindy apply for a budgeting loan for clothes and other household items (especially because the maternity grant would take so long to arrive), but Cindy was turned down because she was too poor to be able to pay back a loan.

Cindy's income allows her no margin for error in her daily expenditure. Every penny is accounted for. From her £31.15 per week, £9.02 is deducted at source by the DSS to pay for her gas consumption. This leaves her with £22.13 per week. From this another £5 per week is spent on cards for the electricity card meter.

This leaves nearly £16 for her shopping, clothes and all her other needs. Over £13 is spent on shopping each week. Cindy keeps a detailed diary of her expenditure:

Beans	27p	Sugar	72p
Tomatoes	32p	Washing-up liquid	48p
Spaghetti	25p	Potatoes	60p
Margarine	54p	Eggs	48p
Lard	42p	Cereals	72p
Bread	1.04p	Rubbish bags	90p
Toilet roll	56p	1 tin Irish stew	64p
Cheese	83p	1 tin meat balls	56p
Soap powder	1.24p	1 tin corned beef	72p
Soap	34p	Other items	99p
Tea bags	72p	Total	£13.34p

Cindy has £2.65 left to spend on all her other needs. Out of this she must also pay 20 per cent of her poll tax.

Cindy's health visitor asked her to identify how much income she needed to afford an adequate diet. Cindy feels she needs double the amount she currently spends on shopping if she is to manage from day to day:

Toilet roll	56p	2 spaghetti	50p
Shampoo	68p	4lb sugar	1.43p
Soap	34p	10lb potatoes	2.38p
Toothpaste	45p	Fresh veg	1.79p
Polish	79p	Fresh meat	5.96p
Jif cleaner	45p	Lard	42p
Washing-up liquid	48p	Margarine	54p
Soap powder	1.24p	Tea	1.18p
Rubbish bags	90p	Fruit juice	83p
3 bread	1.61p	Cheese	72p
Doz eggs	1.07p	Yoghurt	60p
Cereals	72p	Sauces	30p
2 beans	55p		
2 tomatoes	48p	Total	£26.97p

One of the main criticisms of the government's reforms of social security was that no account was taken of how much it actually costs to live adequately from day to day. Cindy survives at the most basic level on her £31.15 weekly income support but her disposable income after doing the weekly shopping is only pennies.

SOURCE: Benefits Research, February 1989. (Figures uprated by the appropriate component of the Retail Price Index between 1988 and 1991.)

It just happened he walked out the time the bills were due. As he went on the Friday they came in over the next two weeks, gas and electric. I get nothing from him, I don't even know where he is. It was so unexpected I'd no time to save up for the bills.[21]

In addition to these initial problems, the woman quoted above subsequently found herself in mortgage arrears. After several months on her own, the lender initiated possession proceedings. She was eventually rehoused by the local authority.

Women and poverty within the household

While many lone mothers are very poor, they are both the recipients and controllers of the resources made available to them.[22] However, several writers have drawn attention to a contrasting position amongst couples, and the importance of considering the allocation and distribution of resources within the household. Several different models of household financial allocation have been suggested, often associated with different levels of income or household circumstances.[23] Amongst low-income households, two models predominate – the whole wage system and the allowance system – but other patterns can also be found within such households.[24] Under the whole wage system, the man hands over his entire wage to the woman who undertakes all financial management (including returning some money to the man for his personal use). In the allowance system, the man may pay particular bills but hands an allowance to his partner for her to manage the remainder of the household's finances (perhaps in conjunction with her own earnings). With regard to these models, an important distinction has been drawn between financial control and financial management. Men generally control and allocate the resources and women undertake the day-to-day management.

For many women, the critical issue is the adequacy of the resources made available to them for day-to-day budgeting. Resources can be inadequate for a number of different reasons. For example, the wages entering the household may be inadequate, even if all are made available to the woman. Alternatively, the resources may be adequate at the point of entry, but the internal allocation may be problematic. Any shortfall in relation to expenditure needs then becomes the woman's responsibility, and may necessitate strategies to 'stretch' the budget. These include many that are by now familiar, as illustrated in the following quotation:

> 'Making ends meet' was cited as the worst aspect ... for a large percentage of the sample and many families were living in real financial hardship... It was often wives who had to live on their wits, variously hunting out bargains, devising new 'economic' meals, locating borrowing sources, placating hungry children, refusing children spending money or treats, patching and mending clothes, going without food or taking less nutritious meals themselves and sometimes dealing with creditors.[25]

Where women need to seek credit or choose to manage the shortfall in resources in this way, their social and economic dependence is likely to restrict their use of credit primarily to the higher cost credit sources – mail order, check trading, instalment credit and money-lenders. In addition, women borrow from family and friends and, if they are claimants, they may apply to the social fund.

Managing debt

Where the allocation of resources is inadequate, the situation will, in all probability, eventually result in debt. Thus, Parker has argued that the roots of debt may lie in the pattern of financial allocation adopted, and the inadequate allocation to women for day-to-day budgeting that pushes them to use credit or miss payments due on service commitments.[26] The influences which help to establish the pattern of allocation adopted, that in turn may result in an inadequate allowance to the woman, have been debated elsewhere.[27] However, one aspect of this process is briefly discussed here. A number of studies have indicated that the internal allocation of resources is informed by a cultural acceptance by both men and women that a portion of the household's money is 'protected' as 'the man's money'.[28] This situation certainly persists while resources are tight, but Parker has shown how even when debts are incurred the 'man's money' remains protected.[29] This situation can therefore also be seen as part of these household financial processes that of themselves worsen an already difficult situation. Resources that might be shifted to the day-to-day budgeting task and to the woman's domain are not transferred. Furthermore, in a number of cases there is evidence of the woman's resources being further eroded as they are seen as available money for the man when he is short.

> He wanted extra money off me which I couldn't give him ... in the end I were saying there was only the £5 electricity money left and he were taking it and spending it.[30]

Other evidence, however, suggests that there may be circumstances under which the traditional protection of the man's money is renegotiated. A study of owner occupiers in default reported that the majority of households effected some reorganisation and reallocation of household finances once debts began to threaten the very maintenance of owner occupation.[31] The reallocations were not equitable, but the inequalities were reduced.

Whatever the form of financial allocation adopted in low-income households, and whether or not it can be argued in particular cases to have contributed to debt, once a household has debts it is likely that the woman will manage them, even to the extent of taking over areas of expenditure outside her normal remit if they are now in arrears. An example, drawn from Parker's case histories, illustrates this point:

> Mrs E had been experiencing financial problems for around three years... Mr E had originally assumed responsibility for paying the rent and fuel bills but had not always done so. In addition, he always kept Mrs E short of housekeeping money... Mrs E had taken a part-time cleaning job to try and improve the household's financial position. This household's indebtedness was not caused by any apparent or objectively measurable lack of money. Mrs E had never known how much her husband earned but suspected with good cause that it was considerably more than he gave her. Neither were the debts caused by any inadequacy or profligacy on

Mrs E's part, yet it was she who had to deal with the unpaid rent
and fuel bills and she who had to seek help. Thus she took on public
responsibility for a situation that was none of her making...[32]

Another case, reported by Brady, makes a related point:

> Yes, I'm usually to blame for it, if something hasn't been paid, then
> I get the blame for it, but it's not my fault.[33]

There are several reasons why debt management is increasingly
'women's work'. Women frequently contract many of the credit
commitments, with the mail-order firm or the check trader who
calls weekly, and they conduct the business with them. In addition,
they may pay the service commitments and when necessary use
that money as proxy credit. Any repayment problems lie within
their domain and are likely to remain so if they are unwilling to
reveal the situation to their partners. Even where commitments
have been the man's responsibility, women may manage them
when they become debts because of their role as day-to-day
financial managers. Here the assumption is that it is they who can
re-jig the budgets and make economies, an assumption women
often confirm, but only by personally bearing the brunt of any
economies. In addition, debt involves negotiating with creditors,
visiting their offices, undertaking to make certain payments.
Women are also often seen as 'free' to undertake this work, either
because their own employment is part-time, or regarded as less
significant than that of the man, or because they are 'at home' all
day involved with tasks that are accorded little priority or prestige.

In Chapter 3 some of the personal anxieties associated with
debt were considered. While it is clear that all household members
experience stress and often feel stigmatised and marginalised by
debt, the position of women as the main financial managers in
households may result in their feeling particularly stressed. Morris
reports that:

> The strain on women was due less to increased physical labour than
> to the psychological strain of being constantly responsible for
> decisions about the allocation of finance, especially in households
> where the man is unemployed.[34]

More recent studies have indicated higher levels of stress amongst women as opposed to men, specifically with regard to debt.[35] All these studies have small samples and the results need to be treated cautiously, but they present a consistent picture. Brady's in-depth study of seven families in debt reported that the women had a higher incidence of self-rated mental health problems than men. He goes on to suggest a group of factors likely to be involved in the generation of stress around the debt problem – the stigma of debt, financial adversity, attempts to cope financially, the guilt and blame associated with 'failure' and the isolation of women. In a study of sixty-seven families with two children living on supplementary benefit, Bradshaw and Holmes used a malaise inventory to assess the general well-being of parents in the sample. They were able to examine the association between malaise scores and other aspects of the families' lives, in particular the level of debt, the length of time unemployed, and income.

> There is no evidence … that malaise is associated with income. Although the longer-term unemployed tend to have higher malaise scores, the correlation is not significant either with male stress or female stress. There is, however, a statistically significant association between the level of indebtedness and female stress.[36]

NOTES
1.   C Glendinning and J Millar, *Women and Poverty,* Wheatsheaf, 1987.
2.   National Council for One Parent Families, Factsheet, 1990.
3.   J Millar, *Poverty and the Lone Parent Family: a challenge to social policy,* Avebury, 1990.
4.   C Oppenheim, *Poverty: The Facts,* CPAG Ltd, 1990.
5.   *See* note 2.
6.   *See* note 3.
7.   *See* note 3.
8.   R Berthoud, *Selective Social Security: analysis of government's plans,* PSI, 1986.
9.   *See* note 4.
10.   S Becker and R Silburn, *The New Poor Clients,* Community Care and Benefits Research Unit, 1990.
11.   *See* note 10.
12.   *See* note 3, and also M Maclean and J Eekelaar, *Children and Divorce: Economic Factors,* Centre for Socio-Legal Studies, University of Oxford, 1983.

13. See, for example, D Marsden, *Mothers Alone: Poverty and the Fatherless Family,* Penguin, 1973, and G Craig and C Glendinning, *The Impact of Social Security Changes: the Views of Families Living in Disadvantaged Areas,* Barnardo's Research and Development, 1990.

14. *See* note 3.

15. Birmingham City Council, *Poverty in Birmingham: A Profile,* BCC, 1987.

16. H Graham, 'Being Poor: Perceptions and Coping Strategies of Lone Mothers', in J Brannen and G Wilson (eds), *Give and Take in Families,* Unwin Hyman, 1987.

17. G Craig, 'Counting the Cost: The Social Fund in Figures', in S Becker and R Silburn, *The New Poor Clients,* Community Care and Benefits Research Unit, 1990.

18. R Berthoud and E Kempson, *Credit and Debt in Britain: First Findings,* Policy Studies Institute, 1990.

19. E Evason, L Allamby and R Woods, *The Deserving and Undeserving Poor,* CPAG (Northern Ireland), 1989.

20. J Tunnard, 'Marriage breakdown and the loss of the owner occupied home', *Roof,* Vol 1, No 2, 1973; O Sullivan, 'Housing movements of the divorced and separated', *Housing Studies,* Vol 1, No 1, 1986; *see* also note 3.

21. Quoted in J Ford, *The Indebted Society,* Routledge, 1988.

22. *See* note 16.

23. J Pahl, 'Patterns of money management within marriage', *Journal of Social Policy,* Vol 9, No 3, 1982.

24. J Bradshaw and H Holmes, *Living on the Edge: A Study of the Living Standards of Families on Benefit in Tyne and Wear,* Tyneside CPAG, 1989.

25. L McKee and C Bell, 'Marital and Family Relations in Times of Male Unemployment', in B Roberts *et al, New Approaches to Economic Life,* Manchester University Press, 1985.

26. G Parker, 'Making Ends Meet: Women, Credit and Debt', in C Glendinning and J Millar, *Women and Poverty in Britain,* Wheatsheaf, 1987.

27. *See* note 26.

28. L Morris, 'Redundancy and patterns of household finance', *The Sociological Review,* New Series, Vol 32, No 3, 1984.

29. *See* note 26.

30. Quoted in C Oppenheim, *Poverty: The Facts,* CPAG Ltd, 1990.

31. J Ford, 'Households, housing and debt', *Social Studies Review,* May 1990.

32. *See* note 26.

33. J Brady, *Living in Debt,* Birmingham Settlement Money Advice Centre, 1987.

34. *See* note 28.

35. *See* note 24 and note 33.

36. *See* note 24.

5. PROTECTION AND SUPPORT

Low-income borrowers face several problems with regard to credit use – limited access, high costs, and, if they default, swift and sometimes harsh recovery processes. This chapter looks at two issues. First, the extent to which the legal and administrative frameworks relating to credit and debt protect households in these areas, and second, the nature and extent of support available to borrowers, particularly from money advice agencies.

The legal framework

The granting of credit is regulated by the Consumer Credit Act of 1974. The Act now covers all forms of credit (except for house purchases), any size of credit agreement and all associated creditors. From the point of view of borrowers, an important concern of the Act is to ensure 'truth in lending'.

The price of credit

The Act does not impose any ceiling on the price of credit, but rather uses two concepts to regulate costs. One is the Annual Percentage Rate (APR) and the other is an 'extortionate credit agreement'. APR provides borrowers with a means of identifying and comparing the costs of different forms of credit. With regard to APR, the Act makes two assumptions – first, that borrowers have some choice regarding their use of credit sources, making comparisons possible; and second, that borrowers will know of, and understand, the concept and as a result be steered away from expensive forms of credit. As far as the poor are concerned, choice was not readily available in the early 1980s. However, the changes seen in the 1980s (the deregulation of credit, the growth in the number of creditors, and a highly competitive market) might have been expected to produce some benefits for low-income borrowers through better access and so greater choice. One of the knock-on effects would then have been a reduction in their reliance on illegal creditors. However, as discussed earlier, there is little evidence to support the idea that poor borrowers have a significantly wider choice of credit sources today than they had in the late 1970s or that they are less reliant on unregulated credit.

The assumption that borrowers know of and understand APR is also questioned by the results of the PAS (1987) survey. One in five respondents did not know what the initials stood for and even fewer could explain the concept. Sixty-two per cent would not even hazard a guess! The youngest and oldest borrowers were the least knowledgeable, as were those in the lower socio-economic groups and the unemployed. Only a third of all respondents said they took APR into consideration when thinking about credit.[1] Protection against excessive pricing via individual assessment of APR is clearly problematic, and particularly so for the poor who are amongst the least knowledgeable and in a position where APR has least relevance.

As the cost of credit rises, some agreements may be regarded as 'extortionate'. The Consumer Credit Act offers protection against such situations by enabling borrowers to bring to court agreements that they believe are extortionate. An agreement is extortionate if it requires payments which are 'grossly exorbitant' or otherwise 'grossly contravene ordinary principles of fair trading'.[2] Following an initiative by a borrower, the court can reopen an agreement, but only after considering several factors – the interest rates prevailing when the bargain was concluded, the borrower's age and experience, the financial pressures experienced by the borrower at the time of the contract, the degree of risk accepted by the creditor, the relationship of creditor to borrower and any other relevant considerations. Borrowers must prove these 'facts', but the onus of proof is on the creditor to show that the agreement was not extortionate. In so far as poorer households have more expensive credit, this process is essentially addressed to protecting them. However, only twenty cases have come to court since the regulations were implemented in 1977.[3]

In the first successful case in 1982 (*Barcabe Ltd v Edwards*), the

APR charged was 319 per cent. The borrower's wife was illiterate and the court were convinced that the borrower had little business capacity. An interest rate of 40 per cent was substituted in the redrawn contract. Many more agreements, however, are upheld as not being extortionate, in part because agreements are considered with reference to those offered by similar lenders. In other words, if all are costly, none is necessarily extortionate.

Currently a proposal is being considered to amend the Consumer Credit Act to allow the court to open a credit agreement of its own accord. Further attention is also being given to the issue of extortionate credit (how extensive it is and whether new means of regulation are needed), initially by the Director General of Fair Trading.[4]

Further protection is, in theory, provided to the poor through the process that allows prosecutions to be brought against creditors trading without a licence. These are typically 'loan sharks', almost certainly charging exorbitant rates of interest but in the absence of any formal loan agreement. It is the absence of this agreement that prohibits their consideration under the extortionate credit process. A small number of prosecutions has been obtained. For example, one local authority consumer protection department prosecuted an illegal money-lender who had offered a woman an 'on the spot' loan of £53 in return for her next welfare payment that amounted to £105.[5] However, obtaining evidence of illegal lending is difficult. In 1978 one consumer protection department reported that 'intimidation and fear ... has resulted in great difficulty in persuading victims to testify in court'. Ten years on, the same authority reported that 'evidence is hard to come by, particularly as the victims of loan sharks fear the possible retribution which may be meted out to them'.[6]

Poor borrowers may also be reluctant to see any avenue of credit closed to them, however costly. As with many forms of expensive credit, legally or illegally offered, the organisation of the marketplace leads to some collusion between poor borrowers and exploitative creditors. For this reason, actions against loan sharks largely come from the authorities. However, the requirements for surveillance and documentation associated with successful prosecutions, and the resources necessary to obtain the evidence, are substantial.[7]

Legislation to preclude overpricing and extortion only provides protection against some of the worst excesses in the credit market, and does little to preclude routine exploitation. As argued earlier, substantial numbers of low-income borrowers may routinely use excessively priced credit. However, given current evidence from the courts, it is unlikely that these costs would be regarded as extortionate and in all probability they would be upheld. Further, there is no protection for low-income borrowers as a group – creditors can continue to offer extortionate credit to other borrowers even as particular agreements are challenged.

Harassment

Creditors generally handle the initial attempts to recover debts themselves outside the judicial framework, using standard letters or personal visits by local agents. If the debt continues, the account may be passed to a commercial debt collection agency. There is evidence that at this stage of the debt collection process harassment can and does occur, despite the fact that it is a criminal offence punishable by a fine. It can also lead to a firm losing its official licence to trade. Harassment includes any threatening language or behaviour, repeated visits or phone calls or other tactics likely to embarrass or distress the debtor. Systematic evidence of the current extent of harassment is lacking, but a number of writers point to its existence. Williams reports that unscrupulous lenders 'intimidate borrowers ... into repayment ... [by] telling neighbours and relatives they are in debt and by persistent calling at the house or constant telephone calls'.[8] In all probability, harassment is concentrated amongst marginal and/or illegal lenders, and directed against poor borrowers. Few cases are brought to court. Again, debtors have to know about the procedure, be able to fund a legal representative and be prepared to close down a line of credit. While there is legislative protection, other factors intervene to render it less of a protection than it might otherwise be.

Judicial debt recovery

Consumer credit debts are also pursued through the courts (often when out-of-court procedures fail). Separate legislation governs the process in England and Wales, Scotland, and Northern Ireland.[9] Despite this, many of the recovery processes are similar, although a small number of important differences do exist. It is not intended to provide a comprehensive review of the legislation, but where common issues are treated in very different ways this is noted.

Actions can be brought by creditors in the county court, typically on consumer credit agreements, and in the magistrates' court, principally for default on rate, and now poll tax, arrears. (In a small number of instances actions can be brought in the High Court.) There are two basic procedures for debt recovery - possession actions and default actions. The former are to recover property (land, houses, goods) where the consumer has defaulted on a payment. The latter enable a creditor to recover sums of money unsecured on land or property. In each case, a summons is issued for the debtor to appear before the court, providing an opportunity for the debtor to make an offer with regard to repayment. This may prevent the possession of the property, or a formal enforcement by some other method of debt collection. However, defaulting on these agreements results in the enforcement of the debt. There are a number of methods of enforcement - for example, a warrant of execution which allows goods to be seized and sold, or an attachment of earnings order. The sanction of imprisonment is available in some situations, including, for example, poll tax default and non-compliance with attachment of earnings orders.

There is considerable debate about the nature of the judicial debt recovery process, and discussion about the direction that any reform should take, and the basis on which decisions should be made.[10] These debates highlight some of the problematic aspects of debt enforcement procedures - in particular, the assumptions underpinning the legislation, the nature of the implementation process and the unequal attention accorded to the interests of debtors and creditors. Together, these and other issues indicate the use of the law primarily to support the creditor rather than to reflect and resolve the potentially diverse circumstances and interests of creditors and borrowers.

Most of the recovery mechanisms available in law are based on the assumption that the debtor won't pay rather than that s/he can't pay. Debtors therefore have to be unremittingly pursued because at best they are incompetent and at worst professional defaulters.[11] In 1980, in a report on debt recovery, the Scottish Law Commission commented:

> It seems likely that the ultimate background threat of enforcement provides a main reason why the credit-worthy pay their debts and honour their obligations... It would be unwise to take steps which, by materially reducing the credibility of these sanctions, would adversely affect the whole basis of credit.[12]

This assumption about the attitudes and circumstances of borrowers results in enforcement procedures being implemented indiscriminately and sometimes inappropriately. For example, warrants of execution to seize and sell can be made against those with few goods that are often of little or no worth and their sale may not raise enough to clear the debt. The potential seizure of goods may also be counter-productive where it encourages debtors to borrow further in an attempt to meet their commitments and retain their property. The use of the bailiffs can also be socially and personally damaging to debtors. In a number of cases, they may be treated roughly, but in other cases the public nature of the process can be intimidating and demeaning. All these procedures continue to be the mechanisms of recovery despite the fact that the empirical evidence challenges many of the assumptions that inform the processes.

Several studies also highlight the limited role accorded to debtors in the court proceedings. As enforcement has become a 'mass' process, administrative considerations have grown:

> ... a debtor attending is an inconvenient spanner in the works of a delicately balanced time machine. If every debtor turned up and had his affairs fully probed, no Judge, in a busy court, would ever get through his list.[13]

Recently, there was a report of a morning's court proceedings where 109 cases of mortgage and rent arrears were dealt with.[14] Each hearing took around thirty seconds. Even where defendants were present, none were asked about their circumstances. The plaintiffs did not have to indicate the steps they had already taken to try and resolve the situation. In circumstances such as these, there is a pressure to apply routine formulae in relation to any repayment agreements sought, and this often results in unrealistic levels of repayment.[15]

The unresolved tensions in the debt recovery process are clear. As debt has increased and creditors have continued to pursue recovery through the courts, either an increased number of cases have to be handled at each sitting or cases delayed. In both instances, the borrower is of little concern. At the same time, there are a number of moves being made – by pressure groups and through discussion documents from the Lord Chancellor's Department – to consider ways in which the role of the debtor can be enhanced and their interests better safeguarded.

It is also the case that an increasing number of people are in debt but without adequate resources for repayment. An important issue is what should be the judicial response to those who clearly cannot repay their debts either currently or in all probability in the future. Here, the use of personal bankruptcy in Scotland, and a certificate of unenforceability in Northern Ireland, offer important contrasts with the situation in England and Wales and potential models for change. (Although personal bankruptcy is possible in England and Wales, it is cumbersome and infrequently used.) The Bankruptcy (Scotland) Act (1985) has as its main provisions that, once debts exceed £750, either the creditor or debtor (or both) can petition the control and distribution of the debtor's assets by a trustee, no new actions against the debtor, safeguards for the debtor and automatic discharge from liabilities after three years. Debt recovery in Northern Ireland is regulated by the Payments for Debts Act (1971) and the Judgements Enforcement Act (1969). The former allows deductions from any statutory benefit for any statutory debt. Conceived as an emergency response to a perceived political threat, the harshest aspects of the Act have been somewhat modified, but still result in a higher level of direct deductions (with associated reductions in income and budgeting flexibility) than found elsewhere in the United Kingdom.[16] The Judgements Enforcement Act provides for an enforcements office (EJO) to which creditors apply once they have a judgement on the debt from the courts. Once the debtor's case is accepted, the EJO interacts with the debtor and decides the appropriate recovery mechanisms. Where the debtor has insufficient means, a certificate of unenforceability can be issued. 'It is technically an act of bankruptcy.'[17]

This brief discussion of the broad legal frameworks that regulate credit and debt recovery has indicated a number of inadequacies with regard to the protection of the interests of low-income borrowers and debtors. Two examples that go some way towards recognising the complete absence of resources amongst some debtors were outlined. However, the law primarily embodies the interests of creditors, providing them with some safeguards against the risks in the market. Support, and a measure of protection for debtors, come largely from outside rather than from within the judicial system, principally through advice agencies. The rest of this chapter looks at one of these forms of support, by briefly considering a number of aspects of money advice.

Supporting the poor – money advice and debt counselling

As the number of people with debts has risen, the need for a free, accessible advice service has also grown. Expertise is needed, for example, to address income maximisation (particularly benefit take-up), to enable borrowers to work out the implications of their commitments, the priorities to be accorded where there is a range of debts and the nature of the approach to creditors. Studies indicate that without advice defaulters often respond inappropriately to these issues, and can inadvertently disadvantage themselves further. Managing debt has also become increasingly complex as the incidence of multiple default has grown. Borrowers may be unable to adjudicate and prioritise the demands of creditors, while creditors may be tempted to compete for the largest share of any available resources. Money advice services developed in response to these needs, but the provision of services has not kept pace with demand. Supporting debtors via money advice still poses some fundamental questions of funding, staffing, availability, and access. 'Independence' and the relationship of money advice services to creditors, borrowers and the courts also remains an issue.

Provision, staffing and funding

The growth of money advice services has been a feature of the 1980s. Sixteen money advice services were identified in 1982. By 1989, specialist money advice was available in 243 locations and in total there were approximately 300 full-time equivalent debt advice workers in the United Kingdom covering both the voluntary and statutory sectors. As shown in Table 12, money advice is delivered through a number of different organisations. Sometimes an outlet is a specialised money advice centre, in other cases the specialist advice is provided from within a general advice agency such as the Citizens Advice Bureau. Money advice services may be provided by local authority departments. In addition to the money advice services identified above, social fund officers are required to provide money advice to claimants. The delivery of money advice services also varies and ranges from face-to-face case work to self-help packs and telephone help lines.

TABLE 12
Number of outlets and staff offering money advice

Providing organisations	Number of outlets providing advice	Full-time equivalent staff
Citizens Advice Bureaux	189	130
Money Advice Support Units	19	39
Local authorities	29	96
Other voluntary agencies	6	30
	243	295

SOURCE: NCC (1990) Survey of Money Advice Services

While the level of provision has grown, it remains parlous when compared to the numbers experiencing debt and debt-related problems. However, any development of the services rests on some expansion and change in the funding process.[18]

TABLE 13
Sources of funding for all money advice initiatives in England and Wales

Type of funder	£	%
local authorities	709,845	50
urban programme	275,443	19
NACAB/local authority	102,995	7
community programme	12,800	1
charitable trusts	56,370	4
private sector	230,000	16
other	40,150	3
Total	£1,427,603	100

SOURCE: NCC (1990) Survey of Money Advice Services

Table 13 summarises the position with regard to the funding of money advice services in 1989, and identifies local authorities as the major funders. Potential developments are discussed in Chapter 6.

Availability, access and independence

Current money advice services are distributed unequally in geographical terms. Large metropolitan areas are better served than outlying regions, both with regard to 'frontline' services (organisations providing client contact) and particularly with regard to the specialist, back-up money advice support units. Of these, there is currently only one in Scotland and there are none in Northern Ireland.[19]

Access is also constrained as demand for money advice exceeds supply. Lengthening queues and waiting periods for advice are a feature of the current situation, and in some places a range of eligibility hurdles has been introduced. For example, specialist agencies may restrict themselves to providing money advice to those with multiple debt; in other cases, 'off the street' access has been replaced by a system of pre-booked appointments and the waiting time can be several weeks. These developments have been necessary even in a situation where it appears that there is still a substantial number of households in debt whose members do not realise they can seek free professional advice, or are reluctant to do so.[20] (Equally, it must be recognised that some debtors will choose not to seek money advice, preferring to rely on their own resources and knowledge.)

One response to growing demand for advice has been some innovation in the types of service provided. This has received additional impetus from the very expensive time commitment associated with the casework approach.[21] Telephone-based advice services and self-help material have been developed – for example, the independent National Debtline. In all voluntary projects, however, the funding base can be insecure. A number of creditors have also established telephone helplines and, in addition, appointed or expanded their employment of 'conciliators'.

A central issue in the provision of money advice services is the question of independent advice. A distinct, but related, issue is that of the perspective adopted towards the debtor. Advice provided by non-creditor organisations can be impartial, seeking the best 'overall' solution that may mean recommending a priority for debts and a lower repayment to any one particular creditor than the creditor her/himself would seek. An important emphasis is given to maximising household income (including benefit entitlements) and to controlling expenditure. The approach may be characterised as 'holistic'. Advice services run by commercial creditors, or social fund officers, raise doubts about the impartiality of the advice provided as by definition they have a primary concern with the recovery of one particular debt. Advice services run by local authorities and situated, for example, in housing departments might also raise similar anxieties, although in practice the evidence indicates that in many cases they have a stronger holistic tendency.

Increasingly, however, the complexities and contradictions inherent in the provision of money advice are being discussed.

From the point of view of poor debtors, there are some tensions centred on the support and expertise offered them on the one hand (that may enable them to retain property or services) and, on the other, the potentially harsh financial regime that may result from the agreements thereby secured with creditors. Others centre on the contradictions inherent in mediation.[22] For example, mediators may improve a client's sense of control over their situation at the same time as enforcing the inequalities and coercive nature of the legal process. In addition, 'a money advice centre can provide vital assistance to debtors who are in immediate need ... on the other hand, it may simply function as a benign form of collection agency appended to the courts'.[23]

The growing variety of forms of money advice (creditor helplines, specialist debt counselling, generalist counselling, independent telephone services, etc) raises the question of effectiveness, and the extent to which they deal with similar constituencies. As yet, little evaluative work has been undertaken. The criteria of effectiveness need discussion. At one level, effectiveness might be closely aligned with efficiency: the number of cases dealt with, or repayment agreements instituted, but, particularly, the number successfully completed. However, in a society where credit use is now the norm (for whatever reason) and debt more frequent, the criteria of effective money advice might be rather differently drawn to include the interests of creditors and debtors in both the short and longer term. Creditors have an interest not just in the immediate recovery of the debt but, where possible, in retaining the borrower within the credit system. Similarly, borrowers wish to solve the immediate problem, but in such a way that further borrowing is not precluded. 'Effective' money advice should strive towards re-establishing routine, unproblematic borrowing, via recovery regimes that are neither socially nor economically punitive. Clearly, for this to be achieved in any substantial measure, other changes are needed in both the credit market and the debt recovery process. Equally, households should not have to enter the credit market solely because they lack adequate resources. A small number of policy initiatives that should be given a high priority are considered in the final chapter.

NOTES

1. Public Attitude Surveys, *The Consumer's Use of Credit,* 1987.
2. Consumer Credit Act, 1974, Sections 137-140.
3. Communication from the Office of Fair Trading.
4. The proposal was put forward in the 1988 White Paper 'Releasing Expertise' (para 6.8.8).
5. B Williams, *Cleaning Up the Debt Environment,* Jubilee Centre, 1989.
6. *See* note 5.
7. S Bolchever, J Stewart and G Clyde, 'Consumer credit: investigating the loan sharks', *The Trading Standards Review,* Vol 98, No 1, 1990.
8. *See* note 5.
9. For example, the Debtors (Scotland) Act 1987, and the Bankruptcy (Scotland) Act 1985; Payments of Debt Act (1971) and the Judgement Enforcement Act (1969) apply to Northern Ireland. In England and Wales a review of debt recovery and enforcement procedures was undertaken as part of the Civil Justice Review. This has led to some proposals and further consultation documents - see, for example, National Consumer Council, *Ordinary Justice,* 1988.
10. *See* note 9. Also, I Ramsay, 'Debtors and Creditors: Themes and Issues', and M Adler, 'Social Research and Legal Reform', in I Ramsay (ed), *Debtors and Creditors,* Professional Books, 1986.
11. P Rock, *Making People Pay,* Routledge, 1973.
12. Scottish Law Commission, 'First Memorandum on Diligence: General Issues and Introduction', Memorandum No 47, 1980.
13. *See* note 11.
14. C Grant, 'Final Demands', *Roof,* Vol 14, No 6, 1990.
15. *See* note 14, and also B Randall, 'Lay before the Court', *Search 5,* Joseph Rowntree Memorial Trust, 1990.
16. M McWilliams and M Morrissey, 'Debt and Debt Management in Northern Ireland', in I Ramsay (ed), *Debtors and Creditors,* Professional Books, 1986.
17. *See* note 16.
18. The issue was addressed by the Ezra Committee, 1990, on the Funding of Money Advice.
19. National Consumer Council, *The Provision of Debt Advice Services,* HMSO, 1990.
20. *See* note 1.
21. *See* note 19.
22. J Davies, 'De-legalisation of Debt Recovery Proceedings: A Socio-legal Study of Money Advice Centres and Administration Orders', in I Ramsay (ed), *Debtors and Creditors,* Professional Books, 1986.
23. *See* note 22.

6. ISSUES AND IMPLICATIONS

The central theme developed in this book has concerned the use of credit and the emergence of debt as a consequence of poverty. This is only one of a number of reasons for credit use, but one that has increased over the 1980s. Most low-income households are not poor because they have taken excessive credit and run up debts; rather they use credit and/or develop debts because they are poor. This chapter examines some of the broader issues raised by the rest of the book and identifies four areas where policy initiatives are required. The initiatives are to a large extent interrelated.

Inadequate resources

While the level of resources available to many households living on benefit or employed in the secondary labour market remains too low to meet basic expenditure requirements, there will be a continuing pressure for them to use credit, not by choice, but of necessity. This is particularly true in households with children. Currently, credit is an important and necessary budgeting tool, often providing financial flexibility, as well as guaranteeing some basic requirements. However, as a result of low income, the outcome is often debt – from a failure both to repay credit commitments and to meet service agreements. For poor households, the solution to debt is an adequate income, not restrictions on credit.

The use of credit by low-income households is, however, currently problematic. Not on grounds of principle, but because the forms of credit available to them are restricted and costly (see Chapter 2). An initiative to examine and design alternative forms of provision is therefore needed.

Low-income credit

Where commercial creditors accept low-income borrowers, they respond to the greater risk by higher charges. With profitability the central motive, no voluntary reduction in these charges can be expected. Any external imposition of a ceiling on interest rates (as exists in some countries) is likely to close down existing avenues of commercial credit to the poor and increase the likelihood of their using illegal extortionate credit.[1] One way of combating extortionate credit is to ensure viable, more attractive alternatives. There is clearly a need for a non-commercial low-cost/low-income credit system. Such a system should be designed on principles derived from an understanding of low-income budgeting processes and priorities. Thus it would have characteristics such as easy access and rapid decisions; small, weekly repayments; the option of personal collection and the facility for renegotiation of payments when budgets were particularly tight. In fact, such a system would have many of the characteristics – save that of cost – that the low-income commercial system currently offers. A low-income credit system should also provide a choice of forms of credit.

Assuming that such a development cannot be commercially based, the issue becomes one of responsibility and funding. The social fund loan system provided by the state has already been discussed, and found wanting in its present form, as it fails in large measure to relate to the principles and process of low-income budgeting. But clearly, a state-funded low-income credit scheme could take a different form. Other countries provide examples of low-cost credit systems organised and funded either by the state or the voluntary sector which should be explored further – for example, mutual loan schemes run by public bodies (eg, the French Crédit Municipal system which lends at below market rates) and state-financed/bank-administered consolidation loans (as found in the Netherlands).[2]

In Britain, such discussion as there has been about a low-cost credit system has tended to look towards the voluntary sector and an expansion of credit unions, and many organisations view them as an important way forward.[3] Indeed, a number of local authorities are actively involved in their development.[4] Undoubtedly they are one component of any low-cost system but as constituted they may not have universal applicability or appeal. For example, they have little to offer those whose incomes prohibit any savings, or those who reject or cannot contribute to a collective community involvement. Other organisational forms and credit structures should therefore also be considered.

It may, however, be the case that the assumption that low-cost credit could not be organised commercially is, under certain circumstances, inappropriate. A small number of initiatives is taking place in other countries (mainly the USA) involving low-income/low-cost commercial banking operations. Often the focus is upon lending for housing or small business development, often in specific communities. These examples suggest that commercial lending to low-income groups can sometimes be profitable and might have a role in a low-cost system.[5]

Debt recovery

While inadequate income and high-cost credit persist, some of those living in or close to poverty will inevitably have debts. In addition to initiatives to address these fundamentals, there are ways in which the protection and support afforded to those in debt could be enhanced. Current judicial and administrative debt-recovery processes serve the creditor, and some (priority) creditors more readily than others, and they are relatively unresponsive to the needs and circumstances of the borrowers. One important issue is the development of recovery systems that are responsive to both creditor and debtor. From the creditor's perspective the need, where possible, to obtain repayment relatively quickly, or to minimise losses (both financial and administrative) where recovery looks unlikely, should be recognised. As far as the borrower is concerned, the recovery process needs to incorporate the reality of their circumstances and knowledge.

For the low-income borrower, one important change would be to reverse the policy that allows the *imposition* of deductions for loan payments and arrears from income and benefits at source. This is a growing trend. For example, social fund loan payments are taken directly from income support payments. Arrears, as well as ongoing payments, for fuel can be directly deducted. An attachment of earnings order instructs employers to deduct debt payments directly from wages. Proposals under discussion will, if implemented, extend this mechanism to a number of other areas.[6] This process has a number of severe disadvantages for low-income households. The amount of money they receive after deductions can be very low and simply necessitate further borrowing. This is particularly the case where the repayment level is not negotiable and set on the high side (for example, as reported with some fuel direct deductions). Borrowers may be charged for the administration of this deduction (as with attachment of earnings), so further reducing their income. The process reduces the borrower's control and flexibility with regard to budgeting, by reducing the number of avenues of 'proxy' credit available to them (see Chapter 2). Where this flexibility exists, it can be a way to stay out of debt.

As a result of publications generated by the Civil Justice Review, a number of potential changes pertaining to judicial debt recovery have received attention.[7] Many of the recommendations made in the NCC's reports, 'Ordinary Justice' and 'Credit and Debt', would be helpful to low-income debtors – for example, that all debts be dealt with by the same mechanism, under the auspices of one judicial institution, with greater use made of procedures such as administration orders that allow all an individual's debts to be managed as one entity; and that debtors receive more support and information about the default process and options by instituting and facilitating lay advocacy within the court system.

Specifically with regard to debtors living in poverty, there is a fundamental issue of the nature of the response where debts are 'beyond recovery', particularly where this looks to be so for the foreseeable future. It must be questionable as to who is served by pursuing debts to the point where recovery processes remove a household's few possessions, or leave them in financial distress, potentially 'recreating' needs and the pressure to borrow again to meet them. Equally, the continuing use of imprisonment for debt (albeit only in certain circumstances), particularly where debts are related to poverty and misfortune (as opposed to any 'criminal' intent), must be questioned. All these points reinforce the need for some priority to be given to establishing a system in which discharge and unenforceability procedures can operate effectively.

Money advice

Chapter 5 discussed the support provided by money advice, the current imbalance between the supply and demand for these services, and the fragile resource base. There is little evidence to suggest that the need for money advice will diminish in the foreseeable future, although its form may change. The question of the responsibility for providing a more secure and adequate funding basis for this work is therefore increasingly important. To date, local authorities have been major providers of the resources. However, creditors have some responsibility to support the casualties of the credit system, variously on the grounds of their propensity to relaxed lending, their social responsibilities and their self-interest. Some creditors have taken or responded to initiatives to fund specific independent money advice agencies or organisations. Attempts to increase and centralise this process can be seen in the development of the Money Advice Trust. Established in late 1990, the Trust aims to raise, distribute and monitor private sector contributions. These initiatives, however, are voluntary and the contribution and continuity they can provide have yet to be demonstrated. Compulsory mechanisms to fund money advice – for example, a levy on creditors – are discussed from time to time and may yet be necessary.

The state also funds money advice, both directly through its grants to a number of advice agencies and indirectly via the provision of funds to local authorities. There is a strong argument that the state should take a greater responsibility both for the provision of the resources to support money advice, and for the evolution of policies to stem the further development of debt. In most cases, money advice is merely a response to the symptoms of an underlying problem. The underlying problems that give rise to much of the debt, particularly in low-income households, have been influenced and structured not only by the policies of some creditors, but centrally by the economic and welfare policies pursued by successive governments in the 1980s. Amongst many factors, the growth of unemployment, the extension of low-paid work and the curtailment of a number of welfare benefits have particularly contributed to a growth in the number of low-income households and to an increase in the number of people who have to seek credit to provide basic goods and manage their budgets. The deregulation of the financial markets ensured that credit was readily available and aggressively marketed. The same low incomes that influenced the take-up of credit also increased the likelihood of debt. Unemployment, in particular, challenged the financial viability of many low-income owner occupiers.

The recent past has been characterised by a growing polarisation in society. For those in secure employment, well-paid and in good housing, the expansion of credit has provided many opportunities and choices, and relatively few problems. Those groups with less secure employment, or no employment at all, have seen their resources and opportunities decline, in relative if not real terms.[8] Credit has been necessary, and often of benefit, but frequently problematic. The number of low-income households in debt has grown. Any reversal of this trend is likely to be closely tied to policies which address the inadequate incomes found in many households, and provide more adequate levels of benefit and an increase in the opportunities for secure, better-paid employment.

NOTES
1. R Simpson, 'Abolishing the Problem', Paper presented to a conference on Unemployment and Debt, Hamburg, 1989.
2. For a further discussion see National Consumer Council, *Credit and Debt: The Consumer Interest*, NCC, 1990.
3. See R Berthoud and T Hinton, *Credit Unions in the United Kingdom*, Policy Studies Institute, 1989, for a discussion of the development and organisation of credit unions. *See* also note 2.
4. For example, Birmingham City Council and Telford.
5. J Shapiro, 'Shorebank Corporation: A Private Sector Banking Initiative to Renew a Distressed Community', Paper presented to a conference on Unemployment and Debt, Hamburg, 1989.
6. For example, in a modified form for maintenance payments from absent parents.
7. Civil Justice Review, series of consultation papers, Lord Chancellor's Department; National Consumer Council, *Ordinary Justice?* and *Credit and Debt*, HMSO, 1990.
8. C Oppenheim, *Poverty: The Facts*, CPAG Ltd, 1990.

Glossary of main forms of credit[1]

Bank overdraft: Flexible borrowing up to a certain ceiling for those with bank accounts, usually without security. Repayments typically over a number of months. Interest fluctuates with base rates but at a higher level.

Bank personal loan: Variable, but fixed-term loan, usually for a specified purpose. Interest rate fixed at the start. Loans can run to several thousands of pounds.

Finance company loan: Personal loan from a finance company. These may be secured on land (houses) or unsecured (for example, for a holiday or a car). Interest rates are generally higher than on bank loans. Secured loans are sometimes referred to as second mortgages when substantial sums are borrowed (usually for home improvements), against the security of the property.

Bank credit card: Access, Barclaycard, etc. Flexible credit facility up to an agreed limit for cash loans and credit purchases from shops that take the cards. Minimum % repayment each month. Currently no interest charges if the total outstanding balance is cleared within a specified time period, but this facility is likely to change. Some cards now involve a basic yearly charge.

Charge card: American Express, etc. Substantial credit facility, but all outstanding credit has to be paid at the end of each month.

Mortgage: Loan from a building society, bank or other mortgage lender for house purchase. Repayment usually spread over 25 years. One of the least expensive forms of credit, with tax relief on the interest payments on the first £30,000 of a mortgage (now at the basic rate of tax only).

Mail order: Catalogue selling with all goods available on credit. Typical repayment period is 20 to 40 weeks. Goods sometimes sold by agents on a commission basis but individuals can deal directly with mail order companies also. Credit is interest-free, but the goods carry a substantial mark-up.

Tallyman (itinerant credit trader, credit draper or clothing club): Doorstep credit, usually for clothes and textiles involving relatively small sums. Fixed interest and fixed repayments often collected weekly on a personal collection basis.

Pawnbroker: Goods are 'pledged' in return for cash. Goods can be redeemed subsequently. Unredeemed pledges are sold in due course.

Money-lender: Cash loan usually between £30 and £1,000 from a local firm (or broker who fixes it with a finance company), usually without security and for a fixed period (anything from days to years); may be paid in fixed instalments or lump sum; interest rate fixed at start.

Credit union: Savings and loan clubs of people with common bond (for example, tenants' association, factory employees), cash loan for particular purpose, not usually more than a few hundred pounds (but could be higher); usually fixed weekly repayments; interest paid on what is still owed at rate fixed at start.

HP (hire purchase): The term used by shoppers and many shops to describe both true hire purchase (where the shopper is in effect hiring the goods, with an option to buy at virtually no extra cost when he has paid all the instalments are paid, and the lender has some rights to repossess the goods as security against default), and the more common credit sale. Usually the shop sells the goods, a finance company pays the shop, and the buyer pays back the finance house, usually in monthly instalments up to two-and-a-half years; interest rate fixed at start.

Shop monthly account: Credit from a particular shop, sometimes to an agreed limit (say, £200), until monthly statement which you have to pay in full; no interest (except in some shops for late payment).

Shop budget account: Credit facility from a particular shop, up to a certain ceiling which is a multiple (say, twenty times) of fixed monthly payments (say, £5); interest, at a rate which may occasionally be changed, charged on what is owed.

Shop option account: Flexible credit facility very similar to credit card, but restricted to one shop or chain of shops and does not permit cash loans. Often with special shop credit card.

Fuel board: Credit for specific appliance, fixed instalment payments, usually quarterly (with fuel bills) over two or two-and-a-half years;

interest rate fixed at start.

Check trading: Document giving credit up to fixed total, usually between £30 and £100, at certain shops; each purchase is deducted from the check, leaving a smaller credit balance; fixed instalments including interest set at start on full value of check usually collected weekly (often in 21 or 22 weeks).

NOTE
1. Some of the items in this Glossary are taken from NCC (1980), *Consumers and Credit.*

Poverty: the facts

Carey Oppenheim

CHILD POVERTY ACTION GROUP

NEW

Poverty: the facts presents the latest statistics on the nature and extent of poverty in the UK. This new and fully updated edition has been much expanded to include fuller coverage of such topics as: debates on the definition of poverty; government and other statistics; causes and consequences of poverty; poverty in relation to race and gender; deprivation in Scotland, Wales, Northern Ireland and in the English regions; international comparisons.

Fully illustrated with graphs, tables, maps and photographs, *Poverty: the facts* is the most comprehensive, authoritative and accessible assessment of poverty in contemporary Britain.

160 pages   0 946744 28 9   £5.95

Please send me .... copy/copies of *Poverty: the facts* at £5.95 each(incl p&p)

I enclose a donation of £.......... towards CPAG's work

I enclose a cheque/PO for £.......... payable to CPAG Ltd

Name ....

Address ....

.... Postcode ....

Please send cash with order to CPAG Ltd, 1-5 Bath Street, London EC1V 9PY

Now's the time to join CPAG!

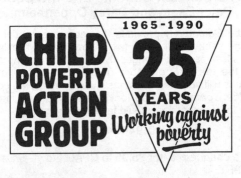

1965-1990
25 YEARS
CHILD POVERTY ACTION GROUP
Working against poverty

We can help you ... with the facts on poverty.
You can help us ... in the fight against poverty.

CPAG membership gives you access to all the latest – on welfare rights, income inequalities, perspectives on policy, and lots more!

And CPAG members give us the support we need to ensure that poverty is at the heart of the agenda, whatever political party is in power.

Send off the form now, and join CPAG in our 25th anniversary year.

Please complete and send to: CPAG, 4th Floor, 1–5 Bath Street, London EC1V 9PY.

- -

I would like to join CPAG as a comprehensive member . . . . ❏
(Comprehensive members receive CPAG's regular journal, *Poverty*, plus welfare rights and social policy publications – £40.

or I would like information about other membership options . . . ❏

I enclose a donation to CPAG of £ . . . . ❏

I enclose a cheque/p.o. (made out to CPAG) for £35 . . . . ❏

Name _____

Organisation (if applicable) _____

Address _____

_____

_____ Postcode _____